"From databases to cultural competency; from dark tourism to emotional labor; from compassion to landscaping. This book shows the hidden work of municipal management in an enjoyably readable format."

Mary E. Guy, *University of Colorado Denver*

"Zavattaro's ground-breaking work shines a light on an area of public service few consider but is vitally connected to all of us – the care of the dead and public cemeteries. With fascinating interviews with city sextons across the US, she highlights the complex management challenges with preserving the memories of the dead, dealing with cultural complexities as communities change, and the critical role of empathy in this unique set of front-line public services. This should be required reading for all interested in developing a nuanced understanding of the full range of public management activities."

Jessica Sowa, *Professor, College of Public Affairs, University of Baltimore*

City Sextons

City sextons are a dying breed and in this book sextons from throughout the United States share their experiences as a city's chief death expert. With a view to investigating their role in local governance processes, how they contribute to public engagement in cities, and what are some misconceptions about this role, Staci M. Zavattaro sheds light on unique public servants that are rarely – if at all – discussed in public administration research. Themes discussed include:

* background stories on each sexton interviewed;
* vignettes of their most interesting stories that can be used as case studies in public administration practice and teaching;
* public history functions;
* self-care strategies they use to deal with the stress of the position.

City Sextons: Tales from Municipal Leaders will be of key interest to scholars studying public management, emotional labor, and leadership.

Staci M. Zavattaro is Associate Professor of Public Administration with the School of Public Administration at the University of Central Florida. Her books include *Cities for Sale*, *Place Branding Through Phases of the Image*, and *Social Media to Government: Theory and Practice* (edited with Dr. Thomas Bryer). She serves as editor-in-chief of the international journal *Administrative Theory & Praxis*. Her work appears in journals such as *Urban Studies*, *Public Administration Review*, *Journal of Place Management and Development*, *Administration & Society*, and *Tourism Management*.

Routledge Research in Public Administration and Public Policy

The Politics of Fracking
Regulatory Policy and Local Community Responses to Environmental Concerns
Sarmistha R. Majumdar

The Data Economy
Implications from Singapore
Sree Kumar, Warren B. Chik, See-Kiong Ng and Sin Gee Teo

Corruption Prevention and Governance in Hong Kong
Ian Scott and Ting Gong

Judicializing the Administrative State
The Rise of the Independent Regulatory Commissions in the United States, 1883–1937
Hiroshi Okayama

State Politics and the Affordable Care Act
Choices and Decisions
Edited by John Charles Morris, Martin K. Mayer II, Robert C. Kenter and Luisa M. Lucero

The Transformative Potential of Participatory Budgeting
Creating an Ideal Democracy
George Robert Bateman Jr

City Sextons
Tales from Municipal Leaders
Staci M. Zavattaro

For more information about this series, please visit: www.routledge.com/Routledge-Research-in-Public-Administration-and-Public-Policy/book-series/RRPAPP

City Sextons
Tales from Municipal Leaders

Staci M. Zavattaro

NEW YORK AND LONDON

First published 2021
by Routledge
52 Vanderbilt Avenue, New York, NY 10017

and by Routledge
2 Park Square, Milton Park, Abingdon, Oxon, OX14 4RN

Routledge is an imprint of the Taylor & Francis Group, an informa business

© 2021 Taylor & Francis

The right of Staci M. Zavattaro to be identified as author of this work
has been asserted by her in accordance with sections 77 and 78 of the
Copyright, Designs and Patents Act 1988.

All rights reserved. No part of this book may be reprinted or
reproduced or utilized in any form or by any electronic, mechanical, or
other means, now known or hereafter invented, including
photocopying and recording, or in any information storage or retrieval
system, without permission in writing from the publishers.

Trademark notice: Product or corporate names may be trademarks or
registered trademarks, and are used only for identification and
explanation without intent to infringe.

Library of Congress Cataloging-in-Publication Data
Names: Zavattaro, Staci M., 1983– author.
Title: City sextons : tales from municipal leaders / Staci M. Zavattaro.
Description: New York, NY : Routledge, 2020. | Series: Routledge
research in public administration and public policy; Volume 25 |
Includes bibliographical references and index. |
Identifiers: LCCN 2020020685 (print) | LCCN 2020020686 (ebook) |
ISBN 9780367250836 (hardback) | ISBN 9780429285967 (ebook) |
ISBN 9781000069754 (adobe pdf) | ISBN 9781000069846 (mobi) |
ISBN 9781000069938 (epub)
Subjects: LCSH: Municipal government. | Public administration.
Classification: LCC JS78 .Z38 2020 (print) | LCC JS78 (ebook) |
DDC 320.8/5092273–dc23
LC record available at https://lccn.loc.gov/2020020685
LC ebook record available at https://lccn.loc.gov/2020020686

ISBN: 978-0-367-25083-6 (hbk)
ISBN: 978-0-429-28596-7 (ebk)

Typeset in Times New Roman
by Wearset Ltd, Boldon, Tyne and Wear

To the sometimes-invisible public servants whose stories I am privileged to learn and tell

To my parents

Contents

	List of Photos	x
	Preface	xi
1	Sextons as Public Servants	1
2	Cemeteries in Everyday Life	9
3	Records Management and Deeds	18
4	Cultural Competency in Cemetery Management	30
5	Dark Tourism and the Cemetery	47
6	Empathy and Beyond	62
7	Cemetery Potpourri	78
8	Concluding Remarks	93
	Index	98

Photos

3.1	Anchorage Living History	26
4.1	Walking Old Chapel Hill Cemetery	31
5.1	Coco's Grave	49
5.2	Don Price giving a cemetery tour	55
5.3	Bangor Cemetery Flags	57
5.4	Halloween Grave	59
7.1	People playing spoons during a festival	89
8.1	Olympic Memorial	94

Preface

I did an interview for this book while sitting on a toilet.

Let me explain.

On September 4, 2019, my dad went into the hospital. My parents live about three hours south of me here in Orlando. They still live in the same town, indeed same condominium where I grew up. I am an only child, and even though I have experienced death in my family (grandparents, a great aunt), I somehow keep a mental block related to my parents dying. We are quite close, and frankly the thought of it makes me queasy still. And this is even though I understand death comes.

My mom called me early evening September 4 to tell me dad was going into the hospital with a urinary tract infection (UTI). No big deal, I thought. Dad has a history of UTIs so I assumed this was going to be another short trip. What happened after that was anything but routine.

My dad somehow went into septic shock. Sepsis is often deadly and is the body's response to infection, often setting off a chain reaction that shuts down the body's organs. My dad apparently got chills and a high fever at the same time, alerting doctors to the septic shock. They immediately brought him to the intensive care unit (ICU). I found much of this out only days after I went home.

I drove home still not knowing all these details and simply packed an overnight bag, thinking he would be in and out of the hospital, and I could support my mom a bit. By the time I arrived, dad was hooked up to what doctors were calling a Christmas tree of antibiotics – large poles holding several bags of medicine. ICU doctors kept telling mom and I that he is extremely sick, asking if we had paperwork indicating if they could resuscitate or not. We had to find the living will to clarify my dad's wishes.

Every doctor you can imagine came in and out of the hospital room – intensivist, cardiologist, nephrologist, infectious disease, pulmonologist, urologist. My mom and I tried to keep at the medical jargon straight, tried to navigate the endless stream of paperwork. My dad would go through phases of improvement and more sickness. It was a crazy rollercoaster that was draining for us all.

xii *Preface*

During those periods of calm, I did two interviews for this book in the hospital. The first was with Bob Nelson from Deadwood, South Dakota. I messed up the dates for our first scheduled interview so there was no way I wanted to cancel again. Dad was more stable at that point, so I took my computer to a small waiting room, put some headphones into my iPhone, and conducted the interview. Bob was so gracious and kind.

The second interview is how I ended up sitting on the toilet in my dad's ICU room bathroom. That interview was with Melissa Haynes from Ruidoso, New Mexico. I decided to sit in my dad's hospital room to do the interview, thinking I would have better luck at a quiet spot rather than a waiting room. Well of course the time Melissa and I were chatting seemed to be when nurses wanted to clean up and change my dad. Someone else wanted to take blood. Because my laptop battery is not strong, I need to plug in.

So, I simply relocated to the bathroom, sat on the toilet, shut the door, and continued with the interview. Why there? Well, it was the closest place I could find that my plug cord will still reach. After we were basically wrapping up, I told Melissa what happened. We both laughed, and thankfully it worked out. That is an interview and experience I will never forget.

At the time I am writing this, my dad is still in a long-term care facility. Mom and I are not sure if he will ever recover fully, and if he does what that means and what it looks like. Will he ever be able to walk again? Will he always need oxygen? These questions might seem silly, but it is strange when your father goes from working and walking to being bed ridden for months.

There was an irony doing these interviews and writing this book while my dad almost died – twice. Many of the sextons told me they wished more people would talk about death, plan for it. When we thought dad was dying the first time, mom and I made cremation arrangements at a local funeral home. The choices were overwhelming. Mom and I picked the most basic package, which itself was not cheap. Funerals, as some of the sextons underscored, are expensive endeavors and often losing propositions for the cities that essentially charge market rate when compared to private companies like my mom and I chose.

It was an honor to do the interviews for this book, talking to such dedicated public servants doing jobs people do not often think exist and often go unnoticed until there is a problem. Any mistakes herein are my own.

1 Sextons as Public Servants

I always considered myself a public servant, but in a different aspect. I always felt like I was a public servant as far as people coming to me in their time of grief and being able to do things that nobody else could do.
(Tonja Walls-Davis, cemetery manager, City of Austin, Texas)

Nobody is happy to see Dawn Ubelaker.

Dawn is both the animal control officer and cemetery manager in Nome, Alaska. Nome is quite remote and is best known for the finish of the famous Iditarod Trail Sled Dog Race. Nome is indeed closer geographically to Russia than to Anchorage. In Nome, they have burial season, as the ground is too frozen to bury during harsh winter months.

When people encounter Dawn, it is usually to remove an animal, to receive a citation for improperly following city ordinances, or to help bury a loved one.

But she would not have it any other way.

"The two jobs just work well together," she said. "Neither one of them takes precedent. I just have a really good balance here."

Dawn has been cemetery manager since 2017, a position the City of Nome had not had previously. The city manager created the job after realizing the burial processes within the city were "outdated" as Dawn described. Prior to her appointment, families were responsible for managing their own dead. They had to report the death to city hall, then file for a permit to dig a grave themselves – or hire someone to dig for them.

A problem was that the city's cemetery records were also out of date, so sometimes there would already be a body buried in the spot a family selected. This happened "more than once" so city officials decided to take over the burial process because there is also no funeral home in Nome.

"One equipment operator started digging, and they actually dug up some-one's arm," Dawn told me. "Bodies up here, for the most part they don't decompose once they're buried because our ground is frozen most of the year. It can be pretty traumatic, right?"

2 *Sextons as Public Servants*

When she took over as manager, one of her first tasks was not only updating the records but also bringing in ground penetrating radar to detect unmarked graves. The radar helped with better updating cemetery records but also "if our current cemetery is pretty much full and we don't know it, we need to know so we can start developing our new land."

The radar survey found 403 anomalies – a likely burial. Each spot was marked with a flag and rebar, and in summer 2018 each got a white grave marker as an indication not to bury there because someone already resides in the space. The grave marker became not only an indicator but a proper memorial for those buried below.

Dawn shared her story with me as part of this research into local government cemetery management. These tales from the crypt keepers shed light on an unexplored area of local government: cemetery management.

Public sector death-care management is more complex than we think, requiring social prowess, economic know how, and cultural competence (Longoria, 2014). Cemeteries are places for reflection, connection, and even education (Francis, Kellaher, & Neophytou, 2000). This book is a collection of stories from cemetery managers throughout the US, in cities big and small, showcasing the many hats they wear when interacting with the public and maintaining overall cemetery operations.

The main takeaway is this: local government cemetery management is complex, ever changing, and heart wrenching. The people who do the job, to me, have something special. For many, they see it as a calling, to help people out of dark times. They also educate the public about a city's history often buried right under their feet. Before delving into the patterns that emerged during data analysis, let me tell you how this book began.

Don Price – Living for the Dead

I was fortunate enough to be part of a research team at the University of Central Florida that spoke with more than 45 City of Orlando (and Orange County) officials after the Pulse shooting, which left 49 people dead on June 12, 2016 in what was then the worst mass shooting in the US. City officials wanted to know how they did – not police, not fire, but city employees such as public works, communications, emergency operations. One of those interviewees was Don Price, the now-retired city sexton.

Don has a southern twang to his speech, and he enjoys living outside city limits and shooting guns at targets on his property. He is generous with his time and knowledge. Don told us about getting a phone call from Mayor Buddy Dyer in the early morning hours after the massacre asking if it is possible to bury 49 people in Greenwood, the city's cemetery. *The New Yorker* published a story about Don, detailing how he picked the location of the plots in the cemetery and his care for the Pulse victims (Spies, 2017). Don told the

Sextons as Public Servants   3

research team not just about Pulse but cemetery operations in general. I found this intriguing.

So, I detour here to share a bit about Don, as he inspired this research. Don began working for the City of Orlando in the 1980s in the archives, going through old meeting minutes from the 1800s and digitizing those by reading them into tape recorders so they could be digitally transformed. "Every day I would sit for hours and read the minutes into a tape recorder, and then at night we'd give it to a court reporter who would stenograph it then convert it into Word and scan it." During that time in the 1980s, the cemetery was under the Parks Department, but city officials decided it should be under archives because of the historical significance. Don helped with archiving some history related to the cemetery and eventually moved his responsibilities solely to Greenwood Cemetery.

"Everybody's life is made up of three things – birthday, death day, and that dash," he said, referring to the line between your birth date and death date on the grave marker. "That dash represents everything you ever did in your life, so you've got to look at not just families, but you've got to look at all of the little things." For Don, the dash is someone's story, how they lived their life. As sexton, Don would get to know those stories for all the families he met.

> Life ends in a minute. I mean, it could end on our way home. I mean it can. You love as you love and you do what you do, but life can end in a minute. So, you learn from the cemetery point that you don't take any day for granted, you don't. It's changed my entire perspective in life doing the cemetery.

When he took the position, Don thought it would be more managerial, focusing on processes, maintenance, and records. While surely the job included all that, he was surprised by how much involvement sextons have with families.

> I would wake up in the morning and go, "You know what? I'm going to help out three or four families today." I would get invited to their birthday parties. I'd be Facebook friended because I was part of their life at this point because not only was I doing the business, I was the keeper of your loved one. I was the keeper. You were entrusting us to make sure that everything was perfect.

He made an interesting point about funeral homes during our conversation. For many families, the funeral home portion of the death process is fleeting – a temporary stop that is focused primarily on the business of dying. With a cemetery, "you're gonna deal with a cemetery for the next 20 years, next

4 Sextons as Public Servants

30 years because you're gonna go and visit. Not only that, your children are going to go to visit." Cemeteries, then, are more personal. This is good and bad because while visiting you might notice if a shrub is overgrown or a stone is out of place, but the cemetery is also a physical location you can go to reconnect with loved ones buried there.

> I always tell people that you're going to usually park in the same location, so you're gonna be able to see 20 feet on each side as you walk so you're gonna be able to see anything out of place. I was like, I want to be the person you come to and say, "You know, something doesn't look right."

When he took over as sexton at Greenwood, his main projects included cleaning up the landscaping and getting the records in shape. He also wanted to ensure cemetery rules and regulations were followed, as the prior manager mostly let visitors have free rein. But yet, in line with other public servants, he knows a lot of discretion is involved when it comes to cemetery management. He told me the story that the person who took over when he retired followed the rules strictly, removing any extra flowers or decorations around grave sites.

Don said a family member "went apeshit" when a stuffed animal was removed from the grave he was visiting. The grave is of the man's 17-year-old daughter killed in a car accident more than 20 years ago. At the time, the family's 21-year-old son was getting married in New York, and the daughter could not get off work to attend, causing the father to fight with her.

> She died that night. The guilt is unbelievable, so he might have an extra stuffed animal, or he might have an extra [flower] but it gets him through the day. He's almost 70 [years old]. He lost his daughter, you know, 20-something years ago. The guilt of having an argument with his daughter the night before she died. I said, "That's what you need to learn about. There's a story behind every death." They went and cleaned all the stuff off of that grave. He went apeshit. He did. And he's threatened everything. You've got to learn his backstory. Now he's lost his wife to cancer. Give that man a fucking stuffed animal.

Don not only knows death through his work but through personal tragedy. He lost his only brother at just 38 years old to colon cancer.

> When I lost him, that was my only brother, and the effect that it had on my mom the effect that it had on my father and everything else, and come to find out he ended up saving my life so there's a lot of guilt, and I see that.

His brother's death saved his life because doctors screened Don for colon cancer given this family history. Doctors usually do not do colon screenings on younger patients but made an exception, and the results of Don's colonoscopy revealed colon cancer as well. "I lost 13 inches of colon. He saved my life. He died, but the only reason insurance would cover my test was because of his diagnosis." Since then, Don has fought other kinds of cancers and won.

Don turned 50 in 2019, and his tattoos represent these moments and memories in life. He has a lot of ink, as he says, but often covers them up because they are intensely personal. Now that he works for sandwich company Jersey Mike's, he especially covers his tattoos as a brand ambassador. But when the art is visible, Don usually does not explain the meanings to people. "I have my own story. Every time that I put a piece of ink on my body it's my story, and I don't have to share it with you or with anybody else."

Just because he is retired as sexton does not mean Don has given up involvement with Greenwood. He has forgotten more Orlando history than most people will know, and he shares that knowledge through regularly monthly moonlight cemetery tours. Tickets are free, and they are some of the hottest in town, selling out in minutes upon release. He also is a regular on WUCF, the local Public Broadcasting System (PBS) affiliate, doing history segments. Walking through Greenwood is a living memorial of the city when Don brings the stories of the dead to life.

Many streets in Orlando are named after people buried in Greenwood. He told me the story of Raymer Maguire (whose street I live pretty close to in Orlando), the founder of Valencia College.

> When he died it was a rainy day, and I'm standing out there, and his wife comes out. I said look you've got 10 spaces right here. I said, I need to know where you want him in these 10 spaces. So, she goes I want him right here. I says, so I'll put you right beside him. She says no, I want to go up here. I said why? She said "because I slept next to that snoring son of a bitch for 60 years, I don't want to spend eternity."

Don personalized every death, every tear. He said he would take the pain home with him, causing him to seek solace in drugs, alcohol, and eventually in meaningful therapy that helped him achieve balance in his life.

> The day I decided to retire was I had a mother come in and she had lost her baby. She had lost like an 8-month old. And then I got a call for the afternoon that a mother had lost her 18-year-old child in a motorcycle accident. At that point I decided I was done. I was 31 years. I was done.

He is the embodiment of a public servant, seeing his role as cemetery sexton to help people, to bring levity in a time of potential tragedy. All the

6   Sextons as Public Servants

cemetery managers to whom I spoke for this research are the same, true public servants only seeking to do good. Don's story got me interested in this unique municipal government function, and I am glad to share some of those stores herein.

This research route is a departure for me, as I normally study local government branding and marketing. This project is one of curiosity, as I also have always been someone who likes visiting old cemeteries. It is a running joke that I will likely find a cemetery in whatever city I visit. When I was attending a conference in Laramie, Wyoming, my doctoral student and I went for a walk to take a break. We found a cemetery, and I detoured us in. He looked at me like I was strange but abided my desire to walk through and look at some stones. In Lausanne, Switzerland I walked to a cemetery I saw on the way to our conference. Another conference on the University of North Carolina Chapel Hill campus had us in a building right across the street from a cemetery, which of course I made my friends visit with me.

Cemetery tourism is not new and often draws people interested in history, culture, or perhaps even a little ghost story (Ravitz, 2009). Taphophiles, as cemetery lovers are called, often travel to cemeteries to learn about the place, the people, and the culture. I had no idea there was a term for something I loved until Don Price called me one. I of course had to Google the term to figure out what he meant. Dark tourism is another way to view this phenomenon of visiting graves, with people drawn to death, dying, and darkness (Stone, 2006). Foley and Lennon (1996) describe dark tourism as the commodification of death, potentially wading into ethical concerns about profiting from and exploiting tragedies. Dark tourism, they argue, is inherently postmodern, with people wanting the simulation of the deceased's life, such as celebrating James Dean's death with period costumes and a procession (Foley & Lennon, 1996).

While out for a walk one day, I kept thinking there could be something more to learn about local government cemetery management. When I checked into the public administration literature, there was not much on the topic, so I decided to go for it. I am indebted to the cemetery managers who spoke to me for this project. I learned so much from each interview and often spoke to people for more than an hour, sometimes two. Beyond the ins and outs of cemetery management, I heard stories about grandchildren going to college, family visits to Florida (everyone likes Orlando!), and much more. Not only was this a project of interest to learn and tell these stories, asking public servants their lived experiences answers Guy's (2019) call to better understand the citizen-state encounter and the intricacies involved therein.

I feel connected to many of the people to whom I spoke, and I am proud to call Don Price my friend. I only hope I do them and their profession justice in these pages. I went in expecting wild stories (and did indeed get some) but learned more about bureaucratic systems, records management, discretion, empathy (and something beyond), and technology use to name a few. The book details the various aspects of local government cemetery management, shedding light on these street-level bureaucrats who seemed thankful someone was asking about their lives and roles. This was such a fun project, and I am glad to share the findings.

When people do meet Dawn Ubelaker at the Nome Municipal Cemetery, her goal is to have them leave happier than when they walked in. She told me a story of one of the first viewings she did as cemetery manager. It was for a woman in her 50s who died unexpectedly. The woman's daughter lived about 500 miles away in Anchorage. There are only local roads in Nome; no major roadways connect Nome and Anchorage. Planes and boats are the best ways to reach Nome. The daughter made her way to Nome and found Dawn's number as the cemetery contact.

"She was absolutely distraught," Dawn said. "She said, 'I want to see her. Can I please see her?' She was crying on the phone." Dawn met the young woman at the morgue facility to arrange the viewing. "She was just so profusely thankful and appreciated that I was doing this for her."

Remember, there is no funeral home in Nome, so the daughter had to take care of everything, and Dawn knew her role was helping the woman mourn in the way she wanted by viewing her mom's body.

> I let her have her space, and at the end she just hugged me, and we just hugged. And she said thank you so much, you don't understand what this means to me. We were both crying. It was a mess.

Mom passed away in the fall as burial season just closed. Dawn said the city tried to get the equipment in to bury the woman, but it was about 20 degrees below zero, and the equipment simply would not work. So, the burial had to wait until June when the ground thawed enough. Until then, bodies are kept in cold storage. The woman had to relive the grief again later in the year, but Dawn was more than happy to be there for support.

"When it comes to helping out your fellow human beings it doesn't really matter to an extent what you're doing," Dawn said. "It's this is what this person needs. If I'm able to provide it, why the heck not?"

References

Foley, M. & Lennon, J.J. (1996). JFK and dark tourism: A fascination with assassination. *International Journal of Heritage Studies*, 2(4), 198–211.

Francis, D., Kellaher, L., & Neophytou, G. (2000). Sustaining cemeteries: The user perspective. *Mortality*, 5(1), 34–52.

Guy, M.E. (2019). Expanding the toolbox: Why the citizen-state encounter demands it. *Public Performance & Management Review*, DOI: https://doi.org/10.1080/15309 576.2019.1677255

8 Sextons as Public Servants

Longoria, T. (2014). Are we all equal at death? Death competence in municipal cemetery management. *Death Studies*, 38, 355–364.

Ravitz, J. (2009). Cemeteries breathe life into tourists. Retrieved from: www.cnn.com/2009/TRAVEL/10/30/graveyard.tourism/index.html

Spies, M. (2017). A graveyard, and a caretaker, for victims of the Pulse massacre. Retrieved from: www.newyorker.com/news/news-desk/a-graveyard-and-a-caretaker-for-victims-of-the-pulse-massacre

Stone, P.R. (2006). A dark tourism spectrum: Towards a typology of death and macabre related tourist sites, attractions, and exhibitions. *Tourism: An International Interdisciplinary Journal*, 54(2), 145–160.

2 Cemeteries in Everyday Life

> I think it's amazing. I love the history behind all of it. The cemetery was kind of one of the first areas of the city in what is considered Bainbridge now.
>
> (Megan Wimberley, City of Bainbridge, Georgia)

In this chapter, I give a brief overview of how cemeteries play a role in our everyday lives. Most are built as giant public parks open for exploration. With genealogy becoming even more popular today with the advent of websites like Ancestry.com or DNA-matching services like 23andMe, cemeteries are main places to trace family roots. (Almost everyone to whom I spoke said helping with this kind of genealogical research is a big part of their jobs.) Full-length books, of course, have been written about cemeteries in general, specific cemeteries, cemetery management, funeral services, and more. The purpose of the chapter is to set cemeteries as a local government function that is often not considered until it is needed.

Greenfield (2011) traces America's first cemetery to Mount Auburn Cemetery in Cambridge, Massachusetts. Before then, there was no central place to bury the dead. Rural family farms or family land, church yards, and potter's fields were popular burial locations (Eggener, 2010). While there also were and still are many ways to handle the dead, Eggener (2010) argues that underground burial and entombment above ground have had the most impact on places architecturally, socially, and geographically. To quote Eggener (2010, para. 4):

> [Cemeteries] also speak of the hopes of the deceased. Because cemeteries are such patently liminal sites – poised between past and future, life and death, material and spiritual, earth and heaven – they more than any other designed landscapes communicate grand social and metaphysical ideas. They offer summations of lives lived and speak of community, the connection to place, mortality, afterlife, and eternity. Serving the needs of both the dead and the living, they are "the identifying sign of a culture."

10 *Cemeteries in Everyday Life*

From a planning perspective, cemeteries as parks are often grand, organized spaces, bringing order to death and possibly giving people access to utopian ideals they could not access in life (Eggener, 2010). The word cemetery was not part of the American lexicon until about the 1830s, and the cemetery spaces represented public places to mourn the dead as well as a push against American exceptionalism and expansion taking place at that time (Sachs, 2010). However, that exceptionalism did seep into cemetery design, with wealthier families showing their fortune with lavish headstones or markers (Pristolas & Acheson, 2017).

Cemeteries themselves are inherently recognizable and unique places given features such as tombstones, greenery, and other markers (Francaviglia, 1971). Cemeteries are usually public spaces and lack a central religious building (Nordh & Evensen, 2018) like a chapel. Family cemeteries on private land often did not have clear patterns of where people were buried, but that changed with the emergence of public cemeteries that usually are laid out logically, perhaps in a grid and with streets and signage (Francaviglia, 1971). Oftentimes, early cemeteries were located on hill tops, and sometimes that pattern still holds today. Many early cemeteries then had the word Mount in their names (Eggener, 2010). Hilltops served not only to give the deceased a potentially good view in the afterlife, but the geographic location also tried to thwart flooding or erosion and stave off disease spread (Francaviglia, 1971).

Sachs (2010) details the romanticism found in early American cemeteries – yet also points out the contrasts found within their borders. Cemeteries are places of death and tragedy, but they also are places to connect, communicate, and relate to loved ones. The physical borders have grounds that are (usually) well maintained, a shelter from the hustle and bustle of developing life in early American times (and even perhaps still today). Visiting the cemetery became an all-day affair for families, and the start of cemetery tourism at Mount Auburn in Massachusetts (Sachs, 2010).

While American cemeteries are still in their relative infancy, death practices and death management have been around for centuries. Burial was originally a mechanism to dispose of the dead but slowly turned into some of the rituals and practices still in place today (Llewellyn, 1998). Cemeteries also were physical places to protect the dead when there was fear of body snatching or corpse defiling (Rugg, 1998). Llewellyn (1998) writes that the word cemetery translates into sleeping place and was a physical geography space associated with Christian practices in early AD times. Many early burials took place in church yards or crypts, but as space ran out there was a need for another place to bury the dead. While Europeans in their cities moved from church burials to cemetery-like spaces, in colonial America the shift went to family farms away from the church, which might have been too far away as the populations grew.

Rural, small cemeteries eventually gave way (though of course they still exist) to the more familiar lawn-park cemeteries globally today (Llewellyn, 1998). In

Cemeteries in Everyday Life 11

the US, that revolution came in the early 1900s thanks to a man named Hubert Eaton, responsible for developing the famed Forest Lawn cemetery in Glendale, California. Eaton supposedly stumbled upon an old, overgrown graveyard one day, leading him to envision a place more pleasant, open, and even beautiful to celebrate the dead (McNamara, 2002). Not only did Eaton revolutionize the physical cemetery spaces themselves but also changed the language around death to be more pleasant – undertaker changed to funeral director, dead changed to deceased (McNamara, 2002). As such, he also ushered in the era of cemetery marketing and the beginning of cemetery tourism, making them both serene burial places and locations for capitalistic endeavors.

Typical "memorial park" cemeteries were often geographically uninteresting, serving only as a functional space to bury the dead rather than one of quiet reflection and commune (Hamscher, 2003). For example, many memorial parks have flat grave markers, as opposed to upright markers, to make mowing and maintenance easier (Hamscher, 2003). Rural cemeteries on the other hand often include more natural, calming features that invite people in. Memorial parks have historically been exclusionary, rooted mainly in Christian memory but many are nondenominational today (Hamscher, 2003).

Sloane (2018) provides a detailed history of the cemetery's changing role in American life. He notes five distinct developments in how Americans mourn that took place since the 1950s: (1) changes in religious faith and beliefs; (2) shifts in our ideas about death and dying; (3) rise of sustainability and a focus on environmental preservation; (4) personalized memorials; and (5) digital media (p. 12). For instance, in America's early days, most cemeteries were small family plots until there was a need for a specific space to fend off disease. As the country became more modernized, there was a focus less on death and dying, and more on medical innovations, literally pushing death out of the home and into hospital institutions (Sloane, 2018).

Sloane's (2018) story is compelling because while he is a public policy scholar, his family also has long, firm roots in the cemetery business dating back to the early 1800s. Sloane's great-great-grandfather was sexton at a cemetery in Ohio, and as of this writing his siblings are cemetery superintendents in New York. Since American cemeteries came about with Mount Auburn, they have changed in scope, service, and presentation to mirror trends Sloane (2018) outlines related to death and dying. During the 19th century in the US, much of death care moved away from families toward privatized industries – hospitals, cities, funeral homes (Searcy, 2014).

The term sexton, which Sloane (2018) and others use, caused a bit of concern among some of the interviewees. One pointedly told me the term is outdated and old fashioned, while others embraced the word and its historical meaning. Sextons were typically affiliated with churches and church graveyards, so many might use the term cemetery manager today. Sexton, though, still represents those who keep and maintain the cemetery spaces. In a Danish

12   *Cemeteries in Everyday Life*

context, for example, sextons are typically affiliated with more rural cemeteries while managers are associated with urban cemeteries (Kjøller, 2012). Throughout the book, I try to use each person's official title but use sexton as an overall descriptor for managing cemetery operations.

Cemeteries are places we can feel a sense of calm and connection to both the living and dead (Ellis, 2003), but this was not always the case in the early days of the US. According to French (1974), many early graveyards were in the center of town and often became dreary and neglected. Poets often wrote sad tales of cemetery spaces, reflecting their place as gloomy and depressing – something to avoid. But Mount Auburn changed all that, making the cemetery into a park-like, tranquil space away from the city center. It was a special place for the dead (French, 1974).

Cemeteries were located on the outskirts of a city not only to stave off disease, but also because municipally owned cemeteries often do not generate revenue so are often seen as a losing proposition for the government (Harvey, 2006). As such, we see large cemeteries on the outskirts but perhaps some smaller cemeteries still located in the city center because there is a reluctance to disinter and move people unless absolutely necessary (Harvey, 2006).

But as our death practices change, there is question about what today counts as a cemetery. Zelinsky (1994) asks if cremated remains in a home or other space count? What about columbaria? Do single graves of famous people count, like George Washington buried at Mount Vernon? Do family plots on a home count as a cemetery? Mapped and named cemeteries are the easiest to identify and study, but there is nuance when it comes to changes in burial practices (Zelinsky, 1994).

Data from the National Funeral Directors Association show the cremation rate in the US for 2019 was projected to be 54.8 percent and burials at 39 percent (National Funeral Directors Association, 2019). This is almost a perfect switch from 2010, when burials made up 53 percent of funeral services and cremations were 40 percent. While cremations are steadily rising, so too is interest in green burials or even virtual memorial services. Nearly 40 percent of respondents indicated interest in green burial services in 2015 (Funeral and Memorial Information Council, 2019). Many of the sextons in my study mentioned these changes in the field.

Like cemeteries themselves, cemetery research is often fragmented and inter-disciplinary. Scholars in fields such as history, landscaping, planning, tourism, geography, business, public health, sociology, archaeology, and others study cemeteries through different lenses (Woodthorpe, 2011). Within public administration, Sloane's (2018) book is the most comprehensive study of cemeteries and their histories. Sloane (2018) uses in-depth case studies of cemeteries where his family has worked or still work. This book introduces into the broader public administration literature the role of the municipal sexton – an often-overlooked public servant.

Cemeteries in Everyday Life 13

Methods and Plan of the Book

After interviewing Don Price, I undertook essentially purposive and snowball sampling to find cemetery sextons or managers from cities throughout the US. I asked sextons to whom I spoke to possibly recommend colleagues who might be interested in participating in this research. For the span of one year, I interviewed 35 sextons from throughout the country. They represent big cities like Boston or Austin, and small towns like Somerset, Kentucky and Lincoln, Massachusetts. They have varying years of experience, from one week on the job to more than 30 years. I stopped interviewing when I felt I hit the point of data saturation (Fusch & Ness, 2015).

Each interview lasted approximately one hour; many lasted longer than that given the interesting conversation. I recorded each conversation for later transcription and took exhaustive typed notes. All sextons work for a local government so are public officials working in their official capacities. I followed coding advice from Miles and Huberman (1994). I did an initial coding of the data to see what patterns emerged, and this was an iterative process. For example, when I began doing interviews, I did not have a specific question about records management, but many of my early interviewees brought up records so I added that as interviews progressed. The same thing happened when it came to deeds, so I adjusted my questions in real time.

Coding was done to organize and understand chunks of information (Miles & Huberman, 1994). Some codes were quite clear – records management, deeds, emotional responses to helping families, maintenance. Digging deeper revealed some of the nuance in those first-level codes. For example, emotional responses yielded secondary codes about taking work home, self-care, and learning as you do. The quotations in each chapter illustrate examples of coding. I gave the codes names and went back through the transcripts once one code emerged (Miles & Huberman, 1994). The process was what Miles and Huberman (1994) call an in-between approach – not totally inductive and not totally a priori. I knew there would be a chapter on records and deeds when almost everyone mentioned those as important aspects of the job. I knew there would be a chapter on helping families, but I did not know the nuance each chapter would need.

It was the dual-minded coding that led to the chapters herein. Because I was so familiar with the data, having done the interviews alone, there could be some bias in my coding, but this is not necessarily a bad thing (Blair, 2015). I was so in tune with the data I knew where some of the information would fall in the coding scheme. The beauty of this kind of project is that others might see something I did not notice at first. For instance, I presented initial findings to my University of Central Florida School of Public Administration colleagues. One asked if culture came up in my interviews. Once he said it, I knew there was another code waiting to emerge that I did not see.

14   *Cemeteries in Everyday Life*

I had plenty of sextons tell me about slave portions of their cemeteries, learning about Jewish funeral customers, and seeing how people from varying backgrounds want to celebrate life and mourn death. That chapter is now included in this book.

A Concluding Thought: This Job is Hard

Many of the sextons told me there is more to the job than meets the eye.

Bill Bibby, the sexton in Charlotte, North Carolina, turned the tables on me. He asked me what I think he does all day at the cemetery. I told him given I have been doing this work my answer might be skewed, so he told me, "Normal people think I sit around. All you do is dig a hole and put somebody in it. I'm like, you have no idea."

For example, Bill talked about government politics. Some of the sextons in this research were appointed by a mayor while others were hired rather than appointed. Those appointed serve at the pleasure of the mayor and could be let go any time. Aside from that, most sextons have small budgets so often must speak up for what they need – or get creative when it comes to finding resources.

> My job is to stick my head out and go to the government building and say, "Hey I'm Bill. I'm the cemetery guy." So I can go to City Council so they know who I am. I can ask for money, but I can't get mad when I don't get it. At least they know who I am. You have to really go out and get it, which I do. I'm kind of the weird guy because people think cemetery guys are quiet, but I'm very vocal because I'm passionate.

He said sometimes city council members (though perhaps not current members) have looked puzzled when they learn the city owns and maintains cemeteries. "Then I will have to tell them, you have seven of them, 220 acres, 500 to 550 burials [a year]," Bill said. He told another story of a council member asking him why a fence line in the cemetery could not be moved – it seemed simple after all to move some fence around. He explained there are actually 20 miles of fencing, and all of it would need to be replaced and moved to seemingly fix that one area. It would cost millions of dollars so there was a workaround done instead – fixing existing fencing during the winter when the grass does not need mowing. He also was able to secure $3.1 million in funding to repair roads and drainage within the cemeteries.

> As a sexton, you have to go get it. You have to be visible. You have to say I'm here or else they will not know. In fact, I've sat with the city manager, I've sat with the mayor. They ask me, "Bill, why am I in the business?" I go, "time out. You are not in the business. You are not in

Cemeteries in Everyday Life 15

the death care business." I said no. Are you gonna give me 10 people to take care of our customers the way they should be taken care of when a death occurs in the family? And they look at me like, no. I said you are in the service industry. We have parks that we bury people in. That is a municipal cemetery. It is not in the private sector where it is a viable cemetery function because they have no idea when it comes to sales.

Christopher Cooke, superintendent of cemeteries in Evansville, Illinois, also spoke about politics.

The challenging part for this role is to be able to navigate the political landscape inside of it because if you don't know how to navigate that mine field you can have all the awards and accolades in the world but your career isn't going to go anywhere. You gotta know how to navigate that mine field, and that's not an easy task to learn. You just gotta pray you have enough opportunities to learn on the job.

He said most political leaders are only thinking as far as the next election, but for him at the cemetery he needs to think strategically and long term. "I have to think about if I plant this tree right here today what's the impact 50 years from now? People in my position, regardless of political background, they have to put the facility above that interest."

Chris Parayno, director of cemeteries and trees in Fall River, Massachusetts, said social media often compounds the political climate for municipal employees and elected officials. He said people in Fall River are quite politically engaged, "which is a good thing. I think people should be politically engaged in government. It also presents a challenge of everything we do is under the microscope." For example, in his role related to trees in town, the department is understaffed for the requests for tree maintenance.

As soon as you go out to a neighborhood and take care of a tree for one person, we've got six or seven calls from the same neighborhood to do more work. We always get threats to go to the paper or put it on social media.

He said people who post on social media or threaten to go to the newspaper are taking advantage of a fair system that sees requests come in and dealt with in an order – first come, first served, essentially. When there is a post from an angry resident on social media,

then I get the phone call from the mayor's office or my boss saying this is on social media and you have to go take care of it today. It does a

16 *Cemeteries in Everyday Life*

disservice because people are waiting their turn, and they get pushed further down the line because of posting on social media. We compound the issue by responding to it right away. People see that is the vehicle that works best. As a municipal employee, it does. The person who posts on Facebook and friends who go to the paper, I have to respond as quickly as possible because it becomes a whole spectacle.

These are but a few examples of the challenges municipal cemetery managers or sextons face each day. Reading along, many of these challenges are similar to what municipal and other government employees face – purchasing requirements, budget constraints, union workers, contracting out, emotional labor, underpaid and overworked, and more. The unique aspect is unearthing how those come together when dealing with the dead, an often-overlooked aspect of municipal government.

As Sloane (2018) notes, the future of death and mourning is changing, and along with that the role of the municipal sexton. As cremation rates keep rising, the body is disappearing from death, quite literally and metaphorically (Sloane, 2018). This is in direct tension with green burial routes, where the body remains front and center. Sextons in my research spoke about challenges related to both burial trends. It is almost wild to imagine a public servant is thinking about what to do with a corpse only wrapped in a shroud. Or how to find funds to build a columbarium to hold cremains, or implementing extended land use policies that allow for multiple burials in one gravesite. But this is the reality for the sextons and something public administration scholars should understand further, along with the general public. Many of the sextons in this work reported not being understood – people cannot understand why someone would want to be around death all day.

References

Blair, E. (2015). A reflexive exploration of two qualitative data coding techniques. *Journal of Methods and Measurement in Social Sciences*, 6(1), 14–29.

Eggener, K. (2010). Building on burial ground. Retrieved from: https://placesjournal.org/article/building-on-burial-ground/?cn-reloaded=1

Ellis, C. (2003). Grave Tending: With Mom at the Cemetery [8 paragraphs]. *Forum Qualitative Sozialforschung/Forum: Qualitative Social Research*, 4(2), Art. 28.

Francaviglia, R.V. (1971). The cemetery as an evolving cultural landscape. *Annals of the Association of American Geographers*, 61(3), 501–509.

French, S. (1974). The cemetery as cultural institution: The establishment of Mount Auburn and the "rural cemetery" movement. *American Quarterly*, 26(1), 37–59.

Funeral and Memorial Information Council (2019). FAMIC study. Retrieved from: www.famic.org/famic-study/

Fusch, P.I. & Ness, L.R. (2015). Are were there yet? Data saturation in qualitative research. *The Qualitative Report*, 20(9), 1408–1416.

Greenfield, R. (2011). Our first public parks: The forgotten history of cemeteries. Retrieved from: www.theatlantic.com/national/archive/2011/03/our-first-public-parks-the-forgotten-history-of-cemeteries/71818/

Hamscher, A.N. (2003). Talking tombstones: History in the cemetery. *Magazine of History*, 17(2), 40–45.

Harvey, T. (2006). Sacred spaces, common places: The cemetery in the contemporary American city. *Geographical Review*, 96(2), 295–312.

Kjøller, C.P. (2012). Managing green spaces of the deceased: Characteristics and dynamics of Danish cemetery administrators. *Urban Foresty & Urban Greening*, 11(3), 339–348.

Llewellyn, J.F. (1998). *A cemetery should be forever: The challenge to managers and directors.* Glendale, CA: Tropico Press.

McNamara, K. (2002). Cultural Anti-Modernism and "The Modern Memorial-Park": Hubert Eaton and the Creation of Forest Lawn. *Canadian Review of American Studies*, 32(3), 301–320.

Miles, M.B. & Huberman, A.M. (1994). *Qualitative data analysis* (2nd ed.). Thousand Oaks, CA: SAGE Publications.

National Funeral Directors Association (2019). Statistics. Retrieved from: www.nfda.org/news/statistics

Nordh, H. & Evensen, K.H. (2018). Qualities and functions ascribed to urban cemeteries across capital cities of Scandinavia. *Urban Forestry & Urban Greening*, 33, 80–91.

Pristolas, J. & Acheson, G. (2017). The evolution of a small town Midwestern cemetery: Using GIS to explore cultural landscape. *Material Culture*, 29(1), 49–77.

Rugg, J. (1998). A Few Remarks on Modern Sepulture: Current Trends and New Directions in Cemetery Research. *Mortality*, 3(2), 111–128.

Sachs, A. (2010). American arcadia: Mount Auburn Cemetery and the nineteenth-century landscape tradition. *Environmental History*, 15, 206–235.

Searcy, E. (2014). The dead belong to the living: Disinterment and custody of dead bodies in the nineteenth-century America. *Journal of Social History*, 48(1), 112–134.

Sloane, D.C. (2018). *Is the cemetery dead?* Chicago: University of Chicago Press.

Woodthorpe, K. (2011). Sustaining the contemporary cemetery: implementing policy alongside conflicting perspectives and purpose. *Mortality*, 16(3), 259–276.

Zelinsky, W. (1994). Gathering places for America's dead: How many, where and why? *Professional Geographer*, 46(1), 29–38.

3 Records Management and Deeds

> In the old cemetery, yea unfortunately we do run across somebody every now and then. Then you just respectfully place them back and scoot over. At one point in time we didn't require vaults. They were in wooden caskets, and they deteriorate.
>
> (Vicki Edson, cemetery department head, City of Elkhart, Indiana)

In the 1980s, all the records for the Town of Edgartown, Massachusetts burned.

A shed where all the town's records were stored burned to the ground, taking the contents into the flames. Not only did that event change how the town manages its overall records, the fire also changed cemetery management there.

Jessica McGroarty is a parks administrator for the town overseeing cemetery management. In the past, she explained the town's cemetery management was always under the purview of a cemetery supervisor. The person in the position did all the administrative work and oversaw cemetery maintenance, but when the cemetery board suggested the seasonal nature of the cemetery lent itself to projects such as records management during the off season, there was a falling out. Edgartown is located on Martha's Vineyard, an island community with huge tourist interest. Seasonal for them means when the island is most populated, so taking advantage of the down times is key.

To fix the destroyed cemetery records, the then-supervisor (who was in the position for more than 30 years before retiring) walked through the cemetery and recorded details from every headstone to build back cemetery records. This process is still ongoing, and it is a big part of Jessica's tasks in her position, which she has had for three years. She splits her time between the parks department and the cemetery.

Right now related to cemetery records,

> everything is in my office. I have that list that was made after the shed burned down in the '80s. That list is hard to work off of because if there wasn't a headstone that person's not on my list.

They use essentially yellow index cards to keep records of who owns the lot, who is buried there, who is allowed to be buried there, death date, and if the remains are cremation or full burial. After the fire, she had to remake all the cards if there was information on the headstone. She had to double check the list with historical records kept in burial books. "I started a new book because the book that I inherited was falling apart. I was like, wow this is from the 1930s so that's in the vault in the [town] Clerk's Office."

They are trying to digitize records, but "we got shot down" by the town council when she asked for additional funding for the project. "I just don't think they thought it was a good use of funds in a tough fiscal year. Every department got shot down." In the interim, Jessica is working with a cemetery foreman to update records. The foreman, who is housed in the highway department, is chiefly responsible for cleaning headstones in the Old West Side Cemetery. While cleaning, he collects data from the headstones and on rainy days will check those notes against what is written in the town's vital records and any other information that might be there to help shore up the records. For Jessica, she must explain to people "we are doing the best we can, but I can't find your relative from the 1700s."

A quick Google search for "cemetery records management" yields many companies that offer services for digital records management. Some sextons in this study reported using a third-party, others have in-house systems, while still others use paper and are transitioning to digital. One can readily see, though, why cemetery records are so important. As the quote to start this chapter shows, there might already be a person buried in a spot that seems empty.

As Cox and Day (2011, p. 89) note, there are many ways to record death:

> obituaries, death certificates, courthouse records, mortality schedules, local history publications, military records, family Bibles, family histories, the Social Security Death Index, funeral home records, tombstones, newspaper articles, internet and genealogy Web sites, historical society files, and genealogy sections in public and private libraries.

Laws dictating records management are relatively recent and even then, there is no standard guide on what to keep and how (Cox & Day, 2011).

A developing trend today is using Geographic Information Systems (GIS) technology to map cemeteries and allow people to use the internet to search records and burials from near or far. A big part of a sexton's job, from my findings, is helping people locate family burial plots or records, so using GIS and digital technologies are becoming keys to this role. Online and digital maps with GPS technologies can allow for a spatial analysis of the area along with a way to pinpoint gravesites (Liebens, 2003).

Dawn Ubelaker is trying to digitize records for the municipal cemetery in Nome, Alaska. Finding records and information of who is buried in the cemetery

20   *Records Management and Deeds*

is an ongoing project, especially with older burials. Still in use are a series of 12 maps on 2-foot by 3-foot pieces of brown paper that she needs to tape together and lay on the floor. She called updating the maps and the records one of the biggest parts of her job, explaining the first obituary on record in Nome dates to 1896. The cemetery was established in the late 1800s, then the gold rush in the area began during the summer of 1900. In addition to those maps, the city also has a cemetery book with names, and each book is used to cross check when someone wants to find an ancestor or loved one buried in the cemetery.

When Dawn began in 2017, she partnered with a cemetery software management company working toward records digitization. During her first winter as the cemetery manager, she devoted a lot of time to inputting information into the system – looking at the maps and book, and transferring names. (It is so cold in Nome that burials cannot take place during the harsh winters so that lends time toward other cemetery operations.)

> As you can imagine, it has taken quite some time with thousands of people buried at our cemetery. It is a slow process, but it is also extremely important.... The cemetery project is ongoing. I am just continuing what others have started, and I'm able to take it to the next level by making everything electronic.

A long-term goal is then taking those digital records and uploading them to a cloud-based system so people can search records from anywhere. When she is out in the cemetery, she makes sure to take an iPad and record any names from grave markers that are not on her existing maps. "The project is just a one-man show," she said.

Lindsay Rhew, the administrative support specialist for the Public Works and Public Space Department in the Town of Hillsborough, North Carolina, said before the city took over managing some local cemeteries, existing records were in "awful shape" because a fire that wiped out some records. "I have a whole drawer full of, like, partial maps, and on those maps we have who is buried there and who owns that plot." The next step is to work with a company to laminate, scan, and preserve those maps via digital copies. Like Dawn, Lindsay also is in the process of digitizing records for the town, a project that could take a few years to even begin due to funding and personnel constraints. There is a digital records management system in place, but it will take time to input information from existing records.

There also are maps that need to be redrawn because, Lindsay said, the:

> maps prior weren't surveyed right. It really is a mess. My first week they told me put these people in the system, and when I tried to put them into the system it said somebody was already buried there. In between rows people are buried. It's not laid out correctly.

Especially in some of the older city cemeteries, the records are not well kept, and the mapping is not right. Couple that with people claiming to own plots but not having the paperwork, "I felt like a detective trying to find out why this man was in this other person's grave. It ended up being his father-in-law he had buried there. We're still trying to figure it out."

Keeping different sets of records is a common theme for many of the sextons in my research. This is not surprising given there should be records redundancy in case of a malfunction. In general, apart from cemeteries, municipal records and public reporting is a vital function for fostering an informed citizenry (Lee, 2006). As digital memorials continue to grow in popularity (Lingel, 2013), online records and access to them will become increasingly important for municipal cemetery management.

Melissa Haynes, the parks and recreation administrative assistant in Ruidoso, New Mexico, said their records procedure is a bit confusing, especially when dealing with two cemeteries. With the city's oldest cemetery, those records went through the county called Lincoln County. The county seat is about 30 miles away from Ruidoso, so that process was not always easy. A problem was that if someone sold a lot and worked through the county rather than the City of Ruidoso, the cemetery staff often did not know if the person showing up to use the lot was the rightful owner without proper paperwork. "When we opened the new cemetery, we said we are not doing to do that."

In the new cemetery, people buying a lot are granted interment rights. The person is purchasing the rights to be buried in the land rather than the land itself, so the city can control the purchasing process. If someone purchases a lot, that is entered into a software that also prints out the interment rights, which people need to sign before it is sent to the billing office. If a person wants to sell the lot, those transfers are then done through the city rather than the county. City administrators, though, do no buy back lots; those are private transactions that must be recorded with the city. At the older cemetery Forest Lawn, Melissa said the individuals still own the property so can sell lots as individuals, and those lots are typically going for about $1,300 a piece – while plots at the new cemetery are comparatively $900.

> I can't just let you go bury your mom or whatever in this lot because you're telling me that you bought it from John Smith in 1962 because there's a lot of things that can go wrong with that if you do. We have to do a disinterment and find somewhere to bury them.

Rights to bury was a common refrain from the cemetery sextons to whom I spoke. This is tricky, though, and usually comes from learning from the past when deeds allowed someone to purchase land rather than purchasing a right to use the land for burial. There also become differences across cemeteries in

22 *Records Management and Deeds*

who takes care of that land – the city, the family, or both? Perpetual care funds also proved a bit tricky for some of the sextons with limited maintenance budgets. Mostly cities use a right to bury rather than selling property that would give a person seemingly unlimited rights to skirt cemetery rules and regulations.

Stan Rogers, the cemetery director in Rome, Georgia, explained it this way:

> They have the rights to bury on the land. That way, we can control no planting trees, no solar rights, and we can do our fire ordinance. We have the authority to do what we think is the best for the cemetery. Everybody that's buried here or every family doesn't have the same taste in mind. And if you go out to [the old] cemetery, you can see the evidence of that. So, what we do is we sell the rights to bury in the city cemeteries. That doesn't mean we're going to just go in there and one day we're going to cover all these graves up and build a store. You don't do that. It gives us the leverage we need to still own the property and maintain it.

Some cities use what are called lot cards. Essentially these are almost index cards that contain pertinent information related to who is buried where. Valerie Fox, the town clerk for Lincoln, Massachusetts, explained their process to me.

> So, say I bought a lot and it's number 14. Then I will draw a card with dimensions of our lot. As you bury people, you might say I'd like to bury my father and I want him on the top left-hand corner. So, I will draw on our little diagram a little box showing the name, date, and details pertaining to the interred person in that area.

In this way, all spaces in a lot are accounted for, allowing whoever comes after Valerie to know if the space in the lot is taken. In Lincoln, as in other municipalities, they allow for the burial of cremains on top of full casket burials. Full burials go down about six feet, while cremains need about two feet per their policies so burials in the lots can be extended to save space.

Vicki Edson from Elkhart, Indiana also uses lot cards. Indeed, her city backs up cemetery records in three different places – the lot cards, computer, and ledger book. She told me it will happen often that a funeral director will call her asking to bury a person next to another in the lot. "It is kind of a mystery you have to solve" when someone might be using a different name than the already deceased, or if the records do not match who owns the lot. The first step, though, is to pull the lot cards to get information and see it matches before going on the hunt.

In Fall River, Massachusetts, Chris Parayno is using lot cards and decedent cards. Decedent cards include the person's name, date of death, date of burial, the location, and the undertaker. The lot cards show where the person is interred within the municipal cemetery. They also allow for cremains to be buried on top of full caskets, allowing up to five people buried in a single grave space. People also purchase rights to bury in Fall River and do not own the land outright. Chris and his team are in the process of generating better digital maps, having completed a drone flyover of the cemetery to better know where an engineer needs to come survey for better records. Once the project is completed – it began in 2016 – Chris said it will allow for people to access digital records anywhere, which will help with genealogical studies and historical preservation.

Digital records have helped Rob Jones from the City of Anchorage move into using QR codes within the cemetery. QR codes (Quick Response codes) are digital bar codes that anyone with a smart phone can scan to retrieve information. The trend of QR codes for cemeteries first became popular in Denmark and some Asian countries before spreading globally (Landsberg, 2018). The digital QR codes and smartphone apps are just ways in which the cemetery is evolving and continues to evolve in a networked era (Sloane, 2018), yet there could be privacy concerns for the deceased's information, but usually the family has to agree what to share, when, and how.

In Anchorage, the QR code is linked to an online memorial, which includes a guest book and obituary. The city does not control the digital content and only offers the service should a family choose. The family gets to decide what content to include and if they want the code open or password protected. "I envision this being a nice opportunity for families to tell more of the story and get visitors to cemetery more engaged in the history of the place." As cremation becomes more popular, Rob said this is a way to include a bunch of information about a person when there is traditionally little to no space on a memorial engraving. Reporters from the *Washington Post* and even one in Germany called to talk with him about the codes, which at first appealed to younger generations but now sees mass appeal across ages. "Nobody outside the building knew it was generating any buzz, and that's okay."

It is probably not surprising that QR codes are making their way into cemetery management as digital, web-based memorials are becoming more popular in today's networked age (Nansen et al., 2017; Sloane, 2018). The digitization is coupled with a cultural fixation upon death, especially those that capture national attention (Nansen et al., 2017). Take Facebook, for instance. Facebook is a social networking site to connect with others, but there is a tricky question of what happens when a person dies? Who runs the account? Can it still be updated after death? Questions such as these prompted Facebook to put out guidance on memorialized accounts. For instance, an account can remain active and be labeled as a memorial, it can be deleted, or it can be updated via a legacy contact (Facebook, 2019). Interestingly, digital

24 *Records Management and Deeds*

memorials such as those on Facebook or other websites seem to extend the connection to the dead, sublimating a traditional death process where communication naturally can no longer exist (Church, 2013). Even though the communication is one-way rather than two-way, there still is a sense of connection that can linger beyond a person's passing.

Historical Struggles and Records Management

It is not surprising that records management and issuing deeds are complex processes. Many of the sextons to whom I spoke manage older, historic cemeteries with sometimes-incomplete records. This is a challenge with historical roots given how people treated and removed bodies has changed through time (Sloane, 2018).

Miller and Rivera (2006) note family cemeteries or rural cemeteries might not have specific grave markings, and oftentimes the body's physical placement into the ground was indicative of the person's social standing. If someone had social standing, for instance, there might be large monuments indicating a family plot; the converse also holds true. They trace a distinct shift in how people were memorialized to the Industrial Revolution coupled with a clearer emphasis on property ownership in the US, thus ensuring cemeteries reflected the cultural and economic landscape of the city, for better or worse.

Cemeteries themselves became better planned usually in a grid format that allowed people to use the spaces as public parks (Miller & Rivera, 2006). Ideally, a grid pattern makes it easier to track who is buried where, though this was not always the case. As cemetery design shifted again to a more rambling layout, records and deeds were of course kept but could be lost to historical changes (Francaviglia, 1971). Records management becomes even more complex in today's age when cremation is on the rise along with extended land use that allows multiple burials in one plot of land (Coutts, Basmajian, & Chapin, 2011). Managers need to be extra careful about marking the records, which is why many of the interviewees reported using redundant records keeping practices such as hard copies and digital.

There seems to be scant research on cemetery records management and deeds specifically. The most detailed article I found comes from Cox and Day (2011). The scholars outline challenges associated with cemetery records management, beginning with noting many states did not always require death registration and family burial grounds often lacked any recordkeeping at all.

> Because there is no governing body dictating standards of record keeping in cemeteries, the nature of these records may vary widely. The information that is recorded and collected from surviving family members can be inconsistent from cemetery to cemetery, and even within the same

Records Management and Deeds 25

cemetery, as time changes and the person responsible for recording the information changes.

(Cox & Day, 2011, p. 89)

A large hurdle in maintaining or updating cemetery records remains personnel time and monetary resources (Cox & Day, 2011). Many cemeteries without digital records often rely on old maps, as I found in my study as well. Some of those precious materials need to be stored in climate-controlled facilities, but that is not often the case. As such, sometimes seeing death records proves difficult so scholars and families are left with the information on the tombstone and little else. Not only are the records vital for historical research and preservation but also for cemetery operations, as records should ideally contain information about burial location, plot ownership, and monetary transactions. Records, then, should be carefully kept and maintained, and given there are no standards, Cox and Day (2011) suggest practitioners seek help from an archivist for proper records retention.

When I did find other mentions of cemetery records and deeds in the literature, they were usually associated with research into rural cemeteries or a brief mention that records and deeds exist. One can seemingly trace interest in the topic to Kniffen (1967) writing about necrogeography, studying cemeteries as geographic spaces of interest. In his short musings, Kniffen (1967) notes cemeteries have rich genealogical records and studying the records and the cemeteries themselves yields an important window to the past for geographers. The most visible record of death is the grave marker that includes, usually, the birth and death date. Necrogeography remains a rich area of study because of the intersecting realities such as the historical record, burial practices, cultural markers on gravestones, public spaces, and more.

Nash (2018) provides a detailed literature review regarding the development of necrogeography. Much of the scholarship, he finds, focuses on origins of headstone materials, weathering rates and pollution's effects on gravestones and cemeteries, gravestones as indicators of other hazards (like invasive plant growth), and environmental effects of burial practices such as embalming and cremation. Cemeteries changed through time, and some crucial records could have been lost as bodies were relocated from rural or family cemeteries to larger burial grounds (Nash, 2018).

Not surprising, the sextons in this research explained they have many people interested in using cemetery records for genealogical purposes. People interested in family histories can turn toward genealogical records to piece together a family tree (Johnston, 1978). As more and more records are digitized, there is a push to couple those with GIS surveys for accurate plots of cemetery spaces available online 24/7, but many of the online cemetery spaces remain static with lists of names rather than searchable features (Liebens, 2003).

Mark Thompson, the parks and recreation director in Paducah, Kentucky, explained "some people are a little strangely enough spooked by the cemetery. To me that's kind of silly. We've got this feeling for history, and it can actually get you a hands-on type of thing." He said he uses Ancestry.com to research figures in the cemetery.

> I can tell you about the cholera outbreak of 1873. I had grandparents who lost four children in 10 days. Those are things that happened throughout the South a lot during 1873 and 1874. You can look through, you go back and you can identify [what happened]. You hear the word consumption a lot, which is really tuberculosis. You don't necessarily see a lot of congestive heart failure. You go back and you see Paducah was actually an area where there was a lot of mosquito-borne diseases because we're kind of swampy and we're down by the river. There was actually malaria outbreaks in Paducah.

Several sextons explained that people in the community use genealogical records to portray living history. For instance, several sextons oversee cemeteries that host community events whereby actors portray historical figures

Photo 3.1 Anchorage Living History.
Source: Photo courtesy Rob Jones, Anchorage, Alaska.

buried in the cemetery and bring those stories to life. The ideal is historical accuracy that seemingly blurs the lines between the living and dead, though the full story can never be realized based on records alone (Handler & Saxton, 1988). It is in this manner that the cemetery can become a post-modern rhetorical expression of the dead, conceived through the lens of the living (Wright, 2005). "The stones serve as triggers for acts of imagination that have little to do with the visual field" (Kelner & Sanders, 2009, p. 140), so people can see the actors yet create their own narratives about the deceased.

Tricia Neal, cemetery manager from Somerset, Kentucky, said,

> I work with our local junior women's club to do a history walk. They have a person standing at the grave dressed as that person would have been from that period. They just basically tell their story as that person. It's not a spooky thing, it's a history thing.

Mark Thompson also has similar activities in Paducah. "They bring back the life that the person who is buried there had and tell about their lives," he explained. He said daytime events usually are for school children, while the same is open to the public at night. An actor might appear from behind a tree to tell the story of a person buried in a nearby grave. "You have to do some digging. Who was this person?"

Such tours are a way to connect with what is gone, to perhaps think about encountering a ghost that continues a city's folklore (Weston, 2016). While ghost tours can fall into the depths of dark tourism (Gentry, 2007), the sextons in my research reiterated the living history tours are meant to achieve a different purpose – connection to the city, the cemetery. Ghost tours appeal to our fear, while living history tours appeal to our knowledge base.

Concluding Remarks

Cemetery records and deeds are vital for continuing success of municipal cemeteries. Cities and towns are already held to strict public records laws, and cemetery records are no different. There often is a time and resource constraint when it comes to cemetery records (Cox & Day, 2011), which is why there is a booming business for online records management systems. What happens, though, is that several of the sextons explained they manually enter each non-digital record when transitioning to such a system. This process is lengthy and often takes years, with many sextons working on the project when they have down time.

Deeds also differ between jurisdictions, but largely the deed allows the owner a right to bury in the cemetery and not a right to owning the land. In this way, cemetery sextons can enforce city cemetery ordinances and keep

28 *Records Management and Deeds*

order. Bill Bibby, the sexton in Charlotte, told me he would almost rather do away with deeds because of the struggles with them.

He explained a city in another state faced a big lawsuit related to a cemetery deed. The city did away with cemetery deeds, but people who purchased a lot many years before thought the deed gave them ownership of the land when it was only a right to bury. "Well there was a lawsuit. A guy buried his wife in a memorial park," meaning the cemetery rules stated all grave markers had to be flat to the ground making mowing and maintenance easier. There could be no upright markers.

> He decided I have a deed, I'm going to put a bench on my wife's property. Well he put that bench in in the middle of the night. The law for that section was flat markers only. He goes, I have a deed and the deed is for my property so I can put whatever I want there. I tell everybody, everybody who has a deed that is the right to be interred in that property. Some of them deeds from the old days, you don't want to read those.

He said his preference would be a simple form that private-sector cemetery managers use. He called it an interment order of authorization, which would be a form getting the okay to bury a person in a certain spot.

> You can have, like, mom and dad bought 10 lots. Mom died. Dad gets remarried, and this new wife has more kids. Talk about those wars, let me tell you. Who's entitled to all the rest of the property? If I'm going to bury somebody, I don't care whose signature it is as long as I get a signature from somebody in that family, they gave me the right to open up that whole gravesite.

References

Church, S.H. (2013). Digital gravescapes: Digital memorializing on Facebook. *The Information Society*, 29(3), 184–189.

Coutts, C., Basmajian, C., & Chapin, T. (2011). Projecting landscapes of death. *Landscape and Urban Planning*, 102, 254–261.

Cox, R.J. & Day, D. (2011). Stories of a pleasant green space: Cemetery records and archives. *Archival Issues*, 33(2), 88–99.

Facebook (2019). Memorialized accounts. Retrieved from: www.facebook.com/help/1506822589577997/

Francaviglia, R.V. (1971). The cemetery as an evolving cultural landscape. *Annals of the Association of American Geographers*, 61(3), 501–509.

Gentry, G.W. (2007). Walking with the dead: The place of ghost walk tourism in Savannah, Georgia. *Southeastern Geographer*, 47(2), 222–238.

Handler, R. & Saxton, W. (1988). Dyssimulation: Reflexivity, narrative, and the quest for authenticity in living history. *Cultural Anthropology*, 3(3), 242–260.

Johnston, A.M. (1978). Genealogy: An approach to history. *The History Teacher*, 11(2), 193–200.

Kelner, S. & Sanders, G. (2009). Beyond the field trip: Teaching tourism through tours. *Teaching Sociology*, 37, 136–150.

Kniffen, F. (1967). Necrogeography in the United States. *Geographical Review*, 57(3), 426–427.

Landsberg, T. (2018). Cemeteries join the digital app age. Retrieved from: dw.com/en/cemeteries-join-the-digital-app-age/a-46450563

Lee, M. (2006). The history of municipal reporting. *International Journal of Public Administration*, 29(4–6), 453–476.

Liebens, J. (2003). Map and database construction for an historic cemetery: Methods and applications. *Historical Archaeology*, 37(4), 56–68.

Lingel, J. (2013). The digital remains: Social media and practices of online grief. *The Information Society*, 29(3), 190–195.

Miller, D.S. & Rivera, J.D. (2006). Hallowed ground, place, and culture. *Space and Culture*, 9(4), 334–350.

Nansen, B., Kohn, T., Arnold, M., van Ryn, L. & Gibbs, M. (2017). Social media and the funeral industry: On the digitization of grief. *Journal of Broadcasting and Electronic Media*, 61(1), 73–89.

Nash, A. (2018). "That this too, too solid flesh would melt …": Necrogeography, gravestones, cemeteries, and deathscapes. *Progress in Physical Geography*, 42(5), 548–565.

Sloane, D.C. (2018). *Is the cemetery dead?* Chicago: University of Chicago Press.

Weston, B.E. (2016). Ghosts and graveyards: Colonial Park Cemetery and memory construction on ghost tours in Savannah, Georgia. Thesis retrieved from: https://library.ndsu.edu/ir/bitstream/handle/10365/27970/Ghosts%20and%20Graveyards%20Colonial%20Park%20Cemetery%20and%20Memory%20Construction%20on%20Ghost%20Tours%20in%20Savannah,%20Georgia.pdf?sequence=1

Wright, E.A. (2005). Rhetorical spaces in memorial places: The cemetery as a rhetorical memory place/space. *Rhetoric Society Quarterly*, 35(4), 51–81.

4 Cultural Competency in Cemetery Management

> People mourn in different ways. You've got all different types of emotions that you have to sit back and see what you're going to get hit with and take it in stride.
>
> (Shane Surber, cemetery foreman, Bozeman, Montana)

Whenever I go visit my Nana and Papa buried inside the Star of David cemetery in South Florida, I place a small rock on their grave to indicate someone came. There seem to be different stories related to why we do this – to keep spirits in this world a bit longer; to warn approaching Jewish priests to stay away from a corpse; stones do not die like flowers; or a nod to a Hebrew word meaning both pebble and bond (My Jewish Learning, 2019). Whichever story might resonate with the individual, all I know is each time we walk through the cemetery to visit my grandparents, my parents and I make sure to find a rock to let them know we came to say hello.

During my interviews, the sextons talked about responding to cultural needs in the cemetery. Cultural competence often comes coupled with having to enforce rules and regulations regarding what items can or cannot be left in the cemetery. This is a tricky balance between allowing people to mourn in ways they see fit while also having to curate a space that is safe for city employees and visitors alike. This chapter details those aspects of local cemetery management.

Cultural Competency in Cemetery Management

Cultural competence is important for cemetery managers because families and loved ones have varied burial practices. Intersectionality adds to this complexity, so cultural competency reflects the ways in which practitioners strive to meaningfully and respectfully engage with people of differing backgrounds and beliefs (Longoria, 2014). Put simply: the municipal cemetery is another frontier to understand social justice issues within public administration.

Debra Lane from the Town of Chapel Hill, North Carolina told me how the town's council decided – without asking her – to sell off some land in one of the town's newer cemeteries to build affordable housing. Lane is an administrative assistant for the town in charge of cemetery operations. Chapel Hill maintains four municipal cemeteries: Old Chapel Hill, Barbee-Hargraves, Chapel Hill Memorial, and Jay Street. The first two are older and have many slave graves. Old Chapel Hill is located on the University of North Carolina Chapel Hill campus, and I had a chance to visit when I attended a conference on campus in 2019.

According to a local news report, the Chapel Hill Cemeteries Advisory Board asked for an expansion of Chapel Hill Memorial in 2013, but instead the town's elected officials decided to sell the land to a company to build affordable housing (Wygant, 2016). What this means, Debra told me, is that traditional burial spaces for full caskets virtually disappeared, making way for a columbarium for cremation burials.

Photo 4.1 Walking Old Chapel Hill Cemetery.

32 *Cultural Competency in Cemetery Management*

Most of the Town of Chapel Hill, they're Northerners. They want more services, and they don't want to pay the taxes. The town is trying to find money, so they got money off the land. They just wanted to get out the cemetery business.

Chapel Hill, though, still has a large African American population, she said. "African Americans don't believe in cremation. There's just something about tradition. They don't want to be burned. They want a casket." As a result, neighboring towns are being flooded with calls about available burial space, which means people who have lived in Chapel Hill nearly all their lives or feel a deep connection to the place might not have a chance to be buried there.

African American funeral and mourning experiences are often public and elaborate and differ throughout the world (Barrett & Heller, 2002). This connection to death and dying might be because African American and black families are more communal, perhaps entrenching closer bonds when compared to white counterparts (Laurie & Neimeyer, 2008). Those complexities become more distinct when adding a religious intersection to the death and mourning processes, so cemetery managers have a tricky job of responding to overall industry changes such as cremation while also being sensitive to cultural needs (Longoria, 2014). Typically, black people believe death is part of the life process so almost embrace it with elaborate public memorials germane to each family. Yet in today's corporatized death industry, preserving these traditions – and preserving black-owned funeral homes – is becoming difficult (Barrett & Heller, 2002; Stanley, 2016).

Dawn Ubelaker works with indigenous populations in Alaska, learning about their cultural norms related to death, mourning, and burial. Nome is a hub for many of the indigenous villagers, with people from Nome often flying in to bring supplies to more remote areas. Anchorage still is the closest place for these villagers to cremate remains, so Dawn helps facilitate transfer of bodies to and from Anchorage. This process, though, can start to back up especially during the winter months when there are no burials.

She told me there are indigenous people living on the remote island of Diomede, which is geographically about two miles from Russia across the Bering Strait. Jelbert (2018) reports many of the indigenous people living on Diomede get most of their supplies flown in from Nome. Traditional burial practices vary by subculture, though often involve community gatherings and above-ground burials given the cold climate (Garber, 1934). Dawn told me they are "not able to bury people in the island because it is just solid rock. People are placed in boxes above ground because they cannot bury." She has helped families whose loved ones have died in Anchorage or Nome relocate bodies back to Diomede, watching as families come together to build wooden boxes in which the casket is placed. "They take care and great pride in how

Cultural Competency in Cemetery Management 33

those bodies are prepared and taken care of once the person has passed. It's an honor to watch some of that stuff."

As populations become more diverse, municipal cemetery managers need to add cultural competency to their growing lists of tasks and responsibilities (Longoria, 2014). Each culture has its own traditions, and for Bill Bibby, the City of Charlotte sexton, learning about these traditions is both a fun and interesting part of his job. "I'm more of a mausoleum person than an in-ground person. That's my preference. But that doesn't mean that's what everybody's preference is," noting that Asian members of his community want to be buried toward the sun, and Jewish people place rocks on graves as noted in this chapter's introduction. "It's not just black and white. It's not."

Cemeteries are an amalgamation of cultural representation and identity – a melting pot even in death. "The cemetery is the appropriate sacred space where the living and the dead are separated and symbolically joined as one people through the performance of transition and memorial rites" (Francis, 2003, p. 223). Though there might be separation based on race, religion, or social status, the result is the same – someone has passed. Memorial practices might vary, but visitors come to feel connected to a loved one. The cemetery, then, is both a social landscape and great equalizer. Physical stone borders or large monuments can distinguish class and race differences (Francis, 2003), making the cemetery a place that not only needs but requires cultural competency, and yet everyone is still physically gone.

Slave Graves in Municipal Cemeteries

Related to cultural competence, I want to detour to discuss slave graves and how the managers in my research spoke about those sites. It was another precarious position to balance contemporary cemetery practices with historical preservation – and a physical acknowledgment of inequities in how people were treated in life and death.

Rural, older cemeteries in the US became an amalgamation of European, African, and new American customs, and for enslaved black people, they relied on stories and memory to incorporate African death, mourning, and burial rituals (King, 2010). Though cultural traditions differed, a common thread was a belief in life after death and wanting to respect and honor the deceased. Enslaved individuals usually waited until nightfall to bury their dead, away from white masters who might stop the funeral and break up the sense of community being created (King, 2010). Some plantation owners, though, wanted to build goodwill so would allow burials to take place on their property and without disruption (King, 2010). (As described later, this was the case with the Somerset Cemetery in Kentucky.)

No matter the context, there is no question there was racial separation in death as in life (Jones, 1999). Just as the slave system disconnected people

34   *Cultural Competency in Cemetery Management*

from land and nature in life, in death those buried were often separated from white counterparts and burial spaces went into disrepair (Jones, 1999). Today, some slave cemeteries are only identified through stones or other rocks marking burial sites, a stark difference when compared to park-like cemeteries in wealthier, whiter parts of town.

Several cemetery managers in my sample were from Deep South cities and spoke openly about this history. Let me start with John Coon, Jr., the superintendent of cemeteries in Selma, Alabama. Coon is a life-long public servant having served in the Air Force and working for government contractors when he retired. (Funny enough, he used to do military simulation and modeling for a company right outside the UCF campus in Orlando, so we chatted about that for a while.) In 2008, Coon returned to Selma where he grew up to take care of his aging mother. "Mom had hobbies. She tried to make her hobbies mine. I didn't want her making my schedule every day, not to be ugly."

So he, like many, started doing genealogy work that took him into one of the city's cemeteries, and while there he learned there was an open secretary position. Coon was in that job for nine years, focusing on records management, selling lots, billing, recording burials, and running the office. The superintendent was there for 39 years before retiring, and he took care of all the outdoor tasks like maintenance and crew management. When we talked, Coon had taken over superintendent duties only eight days prior, after the city's mayor appointed him to the role.

> I'm 72 years old, so I'm not a spring chicken. And I don't plan to be out here until I come out here permanently … I probably really had no idea what it entailed when I first started nine years ago as the secretary. I mean, I knew it was administrative work, and I knew that that was not a problem for me. Whatever that would amount to I figured that was not going to be a problem. I took it just to really basically have something to do. You have to understand our city and our leadership.

Selma, Alabama has a deep-rooted history, often known for the role the city and its people played in many deadly Civil Rights confrontations. There is surely not enough space herein to detail the extensive historical significance of the city, but to understand Coon's story, one needs some context.

Selma is associated with a pivotal event called Bloody Sunday. The Edmund Pettus Bridge was the site of a prominent 1965 civil rights march known as Bloody Sunday. Edmund Pettus was not only a US Senator and Confederate general, but he was also Grand Dragon in the Alabama Ku Klux Klan (Peeples, 2015). The bridge was a physical symbol of white idealism and hatred – a racist message to black community members wanting to live in or visit Selma (Peeples, 2015). In 1965, a group of young black activists organized a peaceful march in favor of voting rights, going from Selma to

Cultural Competency in Cemetery Management 35

Montgomery, Alabama. John Lewis, a longtime member of the US House of Representatives serving Georgia, was then a peaceful marcher brutally beaten, his skull smashed in. Lewis was chairman of the Student Nonviolent Coordinating Committee, which organized student-led non-violent protests (Congressman John Lewis, n.d.), including crossing the Edmund Pettus Bridge. The brutal incident, and widespread images from it, spurred passage of several Civil Rights Era reforms.

Selma is an excellent example of how heritage and dark tourism (elaborated further in the next chapter) collide. Post-Civil War states in the Deep South turned toward marketization of their histories to attract tourist interest and dollars, starting in 1932 Mississippi with "pilgrimages" to see old plantation homes (Eskew, 2001). As Alabama's economy collapsed during the Depression Era, state officials turned toward heritage tourism as a means of historical preservation and indeed exploitation. *Alabama's Black Heritage* was a guided tour throughout several Civil Rights sites throughout the state, including the Sixteenth Street Baptist Church where four young girls were murdered after a bomb ripped through the church, and the Edmund Pettus Bridge. Eskew (2001) details a deliberate attempt to capitalize on black deaths, with officials noting these were experiences tourists could get nowhere else. Today, many of these same sites are part of the state's Civil Rights Trail, which traverses more than 100 spots across 15 states. It is the commodification of civil rights for this generation.

Now back to John Coon and his three cemeteries in Selma. The city owns and maintains New Live Oak, Old Live Oak, and Lorenzo Harrison Memorial Gardens. Old Live Oak pre-dates the Civil War, and New Live Oak is approaching its 100th birthday in 2025. Lorenzo Harrison Memorial Gardens is a black cemetery also dating to the Civil War era. The Gardens had not been properly maintained before the city took over operations, and now Coon spends time figuring out how to fix not only the grounds but the records.

Coon's office is in New Live Oak, and his family roots remain in the city.

> I have family members buried in this cemetery. I know a lot of the people we deal with when their families die. I grew up here. I know these people, at least on the Caucasian side. I don't know many of the African American clients that I have. I know the funeral home operators, but I don't know the African American community as well as I know the Caucasian community.

This, of course, traces to separation of racial communities within Selma and many other cities and towns throughout the US.

Coon is a white man with a deep Southern drawl, proudly talking to me about his nephew attending Mississippi State University where I used to teach. He walked me through a bit of the demographic changes Selma has

36   *Cultural Competency in Cemetery Management*

seen in the last several decades. "The power structure here up through 1965 and the early '70s, I'll just say white and black, and I don't mean any disrespect in any way or the other. Power was white. Black people did not vote" so they had no real voice in leadership, he said. That changed in the 1970s, and the city's current (as of this writing) elected officials are majority black, including the young mayor.

> A lot of the whites have moved out as they retired and had the means to leave here. They have left. We're a predominantly welfare community, a lot of welfare, and I don't mean any of this in a bad kind of way. I'm just telling you how it is. You can Google Selma, Alabama, and the Census data will tell you.

And he is correct. According to population estimates from 2018, Selma's population is 17,886, a 13 percent drop from the 2010 Census figures (US Census Bureau, 2019). The city has about 80 percent black population and 17 percent white, and the median household income is $24,223 (US Census Bureau, 2019). White flight in the city is real.

Politically and economically, the Selma government is suffering. In 2018, city officials laid off 68 government employees due to budget shortfalls and outstanding debt. The layoff resulted not only in lost pay for the individuals but a reduction in government service provision and the temporary closure of some government buildings due to lack of staff (Smith, 2018). For the cemetery operations, Selma went from 14 employees to one: John Coon. His official title is superintendent, but he also is doing his administrative duties and clerk job.

At New Live Oak, Coon has a lot of empty space – but not many spaces left to sell. Why? Well, before fleeing, many white families did pre-planning and purchased plots in New Live Oak, which has the capacity for 20,000 traditional casket burials. Only 1,500 spots remain for purchase, while the other plots remain empty until it is time for burial. Time will tell if the families will come back to use those plots. "Old line families come back," Coon said.

Not only are white families fleeing, black families are as well. Lorenzo Harrison cemetery, which is historically black, used to be called Elmwood. Many black families with history in Selma buried their loved ones there, as the cemeteries were segregated. Records were not well kept, so it became hard to know where someone was buried if other family members wanted to be placed close by. "Going way back, records were not very well kept there ... I don't know how fees were paid." Because of this, only in the last 15 years has the city been able to sell plots inside Lorenzo Harrison. So today if you buy a spot, a deed is issued. Coon said:

> A lot of the burials that we do out there, the family will come and say, "I'd like to be buried next to my mama" and we ask when she died. [We]

Cultural Competency in Cemetery Management 37

ask to show them [the plot inside the cemetery]. If it doesn't look like there is anybody next to the body because there is no marker, our procedure has been we'll start digging, and as long as we don't see any signs that somebody was buried there we will bury there. If there is somebody, we will stop and bury in another place in the cemetery.

Since Coon came on board nine years ago, he has focused on fixing the records at all the city's cemeteries but especially Lorenzo Harrison. This correction, though, is when plots are sold today; historical analysis is much more difficult due to resource constraints. What he would really like is to earn a grant or work with trained volunteers who can look at the markers closely then trace roots of the name on there – if there is a name. "We need some professional people who have the time to go out there or an African American genealogical club that can spend some time helping getting some records on that."

He also has a pipeline of repair projects to fix the conditions, including bringing roads up to good condition and taming overgrown landscaping.

The condition of that cemetery is just not what it ought to be, and it's kind of that community has kind of accepted that that's just the way it is. Well it's not the way it is over here in New Live Oak, and I think we ought to do all we can to get that cemetery out there in better condition.

While Lorenzo Harrison might not be a traditional slave graveyard, many of the burials resembled such with no markers, or decaying markers making it hard to read any names. In Somerset, Kentucky, though, Somerset Cemetery began as a traditional family burial ground, which included the family's slaves. The city took ownership of the cemetery in 2012, managed prior to that by local volunteers and nonprofit organizations. William Fox owned the land and was the first county attorney. "He was a big to do guy around here," said Tricia Neal, the cemetery manager.

"He started his family cemetery on this land," and buried there are himself, his children, grandchildren, and slaves.

He did own slaves, and his children owned slaves. He buried his slaves in the area behind where his family is. Slavery is such a hard thing to talk about because obviously we all know today it's not the right thing to do, but at the time it was just something that was done. You can't deny that. I don't mean to make it sound all flowery and nice, but the fact that he buried them so close to his family was a rare thing, and I think is different than what some other slave owners did. Allegedly those slave graves were at one time marked with little field stones, but we don't have any of those now, so I don't know if somebody removed those at the time.

38 *Cultural Competency in Cemetery Management*

Research supports what Neal told me. Bigman (2014) notes burying slaves nearby a white family and including grave markers was an indication the owners treated the slaves "with more respect than was normal for the period" (p. 17). Interestingly, while slaves were treated poorly in life, death and burial afforded a sort of "freedom" where people potentially include cultural artifacts for the transition to afterlife (Brooks, 2011). Archaeological investigations revealed slave burials on plantations afforded those living without freedom a mechanism to import familiar burial traditions while also creating some for the new world (Jamieson, 1995).

Currently the slave area of Somerset Cemetery looks like it could be empty land because there are no markers, but Neal said people are indeed buried there. In 2018, a member of a local church came out to sanctify the area, sprinkling water to acknowledge the people buried beneath. People who come shopping for grave spaces often see this seemingly empty area and asked to be interred there. Neal of course tells them no. One of her long-term goals is to erect a monument in the section.

> Eventually I do want some type of marker out there saying what it is. There's been several groups come to me and say that they're interested in raising funds to put that marker out there, but it hasn't happened yet.

While not the foundation of the town's cemetery, Margaret Lane cemetery in Hillsborough, North Carolina is an historical slave cemetery dating to 1855. The town took ownership and restored the cemetery in 1987. Lindsay Rhew is an administrative support specialist working for the town, and part of her job is to oversee the cemetery operations. When we spoke, she was only three weeks into her new position and was quickly coming up to speed on all operations.

She told me Margaret Lane is nestled in a neighborhood and kind of unassuming. "If you go out there you don't really think it's a cemetery. There's like one obelisk there and everything else is just green space, and you're like where are all the headstones?" It turns out people stole the headstones to use in foundations when building homes in the 1800s. "The public space manager said people would renovate homes and would find them and donate them back to us. Now we have our headstones back, but we have no idea where the body is or who belongs to who." (The cemetery falls under the town's Public Space division.) The town turned them into a monument wall within the cemetery, so the headstones make up a memorial wall rather than being attached to a specific gravesite. Rhew said:

> It was just such an old cemetery, and I don't know if way back then, it was a slave cemetery, I don't know if that had something to do with it. They felt they could take from it. When the town took over you couldn't

Cultural Competency in Cemetery Management 39

see the ground. It was all so grown up. Now the town has it, and it's this beautiful green space with a couple of monuments and the monument wall. I love that story. I don't know why, but can you imagine going down to your basement to fix something in your house and you find a headstone? I think it's great that they're returning it.

When I was in Chapel Hill, I visited Old Chapel Hill cemetery on the University of North Carolina at Chapel Hill campus and saw the slave section there. The slave graves are closest to a dorm living area and are unassuming. Rocks in the area mark the spaces, and if you did not know any better, you would think these are just rocks dotting the landscape. The town's cemetery board approved "someone to come out and pin every rock so we would know where these people are at rest," Debra Lane said. The slave section was the first area of the cemetery, then townspeople built around it. There is a nice explanation within the cemetery of how preservation efforts took place.

In sum, many older cemeteries throughout the US have slave sections that are often unmarked and unknown. Ground penetrating radar is one tool to uncover these secrets (Jamieson, 1995), though that is generally quite expensive for local government entities. Given that, the best many public servants can do is acknowledge the past by marking the areas as sacred slave grounds. This is an interesting way that social justice fights for equity manifest even in death, as racial segregation usually saw black bodies buried in poorer neighborhoods and away from perhaps-wealthy whites (Francaviglia, 1971). Segregation, then, continued in death as in life.

A Case in Orlando: Pulse Nightclub and Intersectional Realities

I had a long conversation with the now-retired City of Orlando sexton Don Price. Greenwood Cemetery, too, has a slave section with many unmarked graves, but here I tell you about how Price handled burying victims of the Pulse nightclub shooting tragedy that left 49 people dead in the early morning hours of June 12, 2016. Pulse was an LGBTQ nightclub, and that evening was Latin night. At the time, the Pulse massacre was the worst mass shooting in the US, sadly beat out later by the killings in Las Vegas.

Price was appointed sexton in the early 2000s (he told me it was either 2003 or 2004), then went to mortuary school to learn more.

The most impressive thing I ever learned is one of my instructors goes, "You know, they can trace a drop of blood form your fingertip through your entire body he said, but I can't tell you what to say sitting across the table from a mother who just lost her child." He said scientifically I can tell you everything you need to know but personally I can't tell you. So

40   *Cultural Competency in Cemetery Management*

> that made a big impact on my life that I'm dealing with families, and I'm dealing with everything else.

While Price dealt with death and dying as sexton for more than 30 years, Pulse was one of his biggest challenges.

> I was sitting at Cape Canaveral watching a rocket go up, and then I get a phone call from the mayor that 49 people, at that point they didn't know, but all these people were killed at Pulse so I had to come home right away. Right away.

That call came early Monday morning from Mayor Buddy Dyer, asking Don about burying victims in Greenwood and warning him what was coming given the magnitude of the massacre.

The Pulse scene was one of chaos and ever-changing conditions. There are many news articles and after-action reports about the incident, but my focus here is on Price and his role at the cemetery. As noted, Pulse was an LGBTQ nightclub, so for Price he was helping victims' families who might not have known their loved one identified as LGBTQ+. Many of the victims that night were young – teenagers or early 20s – and many survivors, Price said, had never directly dealt with death. "You're just getting beaten," he explained.

Price had many tasks following Pulse, including ensuring people were not being price gouged by funeral-related companies. State officials also were involved, wanting to keep pricing fair given the circumstances. For instance, he said 21 victims were flown to Puerto Rico for burial (as a reminder it was Latin night as well in the club, so there were myriad intersectional identities and some victims had families in other countries),

> so kind of like with a hurricane where you make sure that everybody's being treated fairly. We had to track every single one of those bodies to make sure that they were being treated correctly, that the funeral homes weren't jacking up prices.

At Greenwood, Price had to make sure the funerals there went smoothly. That meant handling the media, mourners, and even protestors. The city donated funeral plots for the victims buried inside Greenwood; currently four Pulse victims are buried there (Montero, 2016). Orlando City Council members in 2019 approved a permanent memorial inside Greenwood consisting of seven rows of seven stones to memorialize the 49 victims. Additionally, 12 grave spaces will remain available until 2024 for Pulse victims' families (Seabrook, 2019), though there are spots set aside for all victims in case bodies need to be returned from overseas cemeteries (Peters & Cavacini, 2019).

Cultural Competency in Cemetery Management   41

During one of the funeral services, Price said he met someone who identified as a transvestite who "never in her life has dealt with death. Never. I'm talking to her at funerals, and she's just out there from a distance." She was a performer at another Orlando gay club, so Price said she knew many of the victims, though perhaps not personally but through shared experiences at the nightclubs. Not only was she experiencing death for the first time, but:

> she had to deal with 49. So we sat there and talked for a while, and she couldn't understand the magnitude because not only 49 died, we had many more who were injured. These are humans. She gave me this whole new perspective on life.… She never lost a parent, she never lost a grandparent. These were the first funerals she's ever been to. It killed me inside, it really did. It killed me. Here she was standing from a distance because she couldn't approach the gravesites.

During Price's 31 years, he saw a lot of death – including a person committing suicide right outside his office in Greenwood. He takes all of those personally. "Pulse hit me hard. It did because these were kids," he told me. Westboro Baptist Church members, known for their anti-LGBTQ rhetoric and general hatred, were rumored to protest outside funerals so Price took extra measures to safeguard the cemetery, pulling a parade permit so he could shut down streets and cover the street-facing fences near the services with dark screens and rainbow flags (Spies, 2017).

This instance shows how municipal cemetery managers are always changing and learning. Regarding Pulse, the victims were Latinx and LGBTQ identifying, so those intersectional realities are something all city officials coming in contact with victims and victims' families needed to learn and listen.

Funeral Economics

Another social justice challenge manifesting in the cemetery is the cost. In the preface, I mentioned purchasing a cremation package for my father when we thought he was going to die. The cheapest package we found at the funeral home we used was about $2,500. I put the down payment, and my mom is going to make smaller monthly payments. To say we had sticker shock is an understatement.

Longoria (2014) finds residents in Austin, Texas are paying unequal amounts for death care given economic disparities. He finds the median White family household will spend about 16 percent of their annual income on funeral costs, while African American households could be expected to pay up to nearly 27 percent and Latino households hover about 22 percent. "The burden on some families is severe, and some families take on excessive debt,

42 *Cultural Competency in Cemetery Management*

borrowing money from family, or hold fundraisers to pay costs and uphold perceived cultural expectations" (Longoria, 2014, p. 362).

Melissa Haynes in Ruidoso, New Mexico told me city plots cost $900 and burial costs are another $900, not including the casket, funeral service, and cremation if the family chooses that route.

> We don't take payments. That's one thing that I personally struggle with. I just think that it's very expensive to die. But I don't know the answer. I'm not sure what other people do with that. We don't have the means to keep track of someone making 100 payments on lots here and there.

It is perhaps not surprising that death is a consumer product. There are so many options – kinds of caskets and urns, the service itself, opening costs, closing costs, renting a space for a celebration of life, etc. The bigger the funeral and memorial, the more likely someone is to have money and status (Pine & Phillips, 1970). Funerals, then, are performative acts where a family might want to signify grandeur in death even if there was little in life.

The social justice problem of financial resources is exacerbated as the funeral home industry becomes more centralized and even monopolized (Drakeford, 1998). The sextons in this research told me they are not subject to those pressures to sell, sell, sell. Indeed, they are public servants who offer spaces and fair market prices. Usually they will do a comparative analysis of other nearby cities to ensure they are still competitive but cannot charge prices that necessarily generate profit.

Shane Surber, cemetery foreman in Bozeman, Montana, said,

> I find it interesting to call around and see what other people are charging. He said fees in Bozeman for a plot are about $1,500, and while it is relatively inexpensive compared to other states, when compared to other cities nearby it could be considered expensive.

His department, though, is being tasked with making more money so one way they are doing that is through a scattering garden plaque rather than a headstone. They tried selling flowers, but that did not yield a lot of revenue. "A perennial problem is time, resources, and staffing. I think we are doing pretty well though. Everybody is happy."

Craig Hudson in Auburn, Washington, told me his city offers a variety of choices for people when it comes to funerals and memorials. He told me a story about a newer area of the cemetery called ForestWalk, a more nature-based space offering a variety of burial options. In 2012, the city added a water fountain feature to ForestWalk, complete with a Koi pond and urn spaces that overlook nearby mountains. "It's kind of a blue-collar town. We've got probably about 80,000 people in Auburn here."

When that section of ForestWalk opened with the water feature, Craig said they were not sure what price point to set. There are cremation spaces next to the stream, "and the first day we opened I think I sold three $4,000 cremation plots ... It was like, wow, okay, people like water. If you build it they will come type of thing." He said there also is a wishing well, and families can scatter ashes using fluid from the well. That option costs about $700 including fees. "We've tried to be able to help families that might not have a lot of money, and we just have a lot of options for both cremation and traditional."

Anchorage Memorial Park Cemetery is a bit different, Rob Jones told me. He said the city does not charge for burial spaces because President Woodrow Wilson declared the land to be free for public burial. As the city's website details, President Wilson issued two executive orders, one establishing a cemetery reserve area for Anchorage and another indicating burial land should be made available for free to the public (Municipality of Anchorage, 2019). The orders also authorized half the land to be set aside for ownership by private religious institutions, which still holds true today (Municipality of Anchorage, 2019). While the city does not charge people for land, it does charge other fees such as opening and closing, interment and disinterment, and niche spaces. "Ours is by far the least expensive at least initially because we don't sell the land," Rob said about the cemetery when compared to others in Anchorage.

> I still don't know why he (President Wilson) thought that our tent city needed a 22-acre cemetery at the time, but his wife had recently passed and he may have had that experience that people don't have to rely on until they're actually in it.

It is a tough spot for many cemetery managers because cemetery perpetual care is expensive – and often a losing proposition. It is expensive to mow, plant trees, maintain roadways, maintain walls and fences, clean the property, manage records, pay people, etc. Though cities cannot charge more than fair prices, a limitation compared to private sector counterparts who can alter fee structures almost at a whim. The sextons need to follow purchasing provisions when they need new equipment. Most have set budgets that allow them to get by each year, but that means there is not a lot of wiggle room if something goes wrong or if they want to try something new.

Richard Gerbasi, the cemetery director for the City of Savannah, Georgia, summed this point up nicely about cemetery services:

> I could easily triple prices to try to close that [budget] gap, but I'd be doing a disservice to the community, and at the end of the day it's not about how much profit we can make. It's we provide the service to the community, and we're also preserving the culture and the history of the

44 *Cultural Competency in Cemetery Management*

city and its people. And it's going to last forever. It's a place for many purposes.

Concluding Thoughts

Many of the sextons in this research mentioned learning about different cultures and burial customs. They also reported struggling with the financial aspects of funerals – burials are expensive, but they cannot simply raise prices unfairly given the public service mission. Just as individuals mourn differently, adding cultural considerations also creates another intersectional layer for cemetery managers to understand. This is tied to empathy and understanding, being able to listen and give people what they need. As our overall cultural relationship with death changes, so too do traditional mourning practices (Parkes, Laungani, & Young, 2015). And yet for many cultures, these death and mourning practices remain at the center of how one handles death.

As Walter (2015) notes, death practices in the US were traditionally rooted in Christian beliefs, but as society changed those practices became largely secular. Now, this is not to say religion no longer plays a role in death and dying – surely religion for many is at the center for those practices. But according to Walter (2015), as society in general becomes more secular and perhaps spiritual rather than religious, it makes sense for death practices to follow. With cremation becoming more popular, it removes the physical body from the mourning space, and ceremonies that once focused on mourning now celebrate life (Walter, 2017).

Long and Buehring (2014, p. 80) sum cultural changes up this way:

> Even a cursory look at the obituary section of the local newspaper suggests that urban Americans practice a wide range of mortuary customs. There are private services and large public gatherings, services at churches, funeral homes or cemeteries. Others memorial events might be held at nursing homes or restaurants. Or, there may be no service until further notice, perhaps none at all. Mourners and friends may attend in person or by streaming video; they may send flowers, or donate to a charity in lieu of flowers, or pray for the soul of the departed. Bodies may be embalmed or frozen, buried or burned, ashes scattered or gathered into jars. When a family member died almost 30 years ago, the big decision was what she should be wearing for the "viewing" of the corpse at the wake, but today there are more choices and more decisions to be made, including even the possibility of a pre-death party where the dying person can celebrate with friends and family while still alive.

Municipal sextons need to handle changing social conditions surrounding death, changing burial practices, incoming technological shifts, and intersecting

Cultural Competency in Cemetery Management   45

cultural identities. This adds another layer to municipal cemetery management that public servants in other roles might not have to consider as closely.

References

Barrett, R.K. & Heller, K.S. (2002). Death and dying in the black experience. *Journal of Palliative Medicine*, 5(5), 793–799.

Bigman, D.P. (2014). Mapping social relationships: Geophysical survey of a nineteenth-century American slave cemetery. *Archaeological and Anthropological Sciences*, 6(1), 17–30.

Brooks, C. (2011). Enclosing their immortal souls: A survey of two African American cemeteries in Georgetown, South Carolina. *Southeastern Archaeology*, 30(1), 176–186.

Congressman John Lewis (n.d.). Biography. Retrieved from: https://johnlewis.house.gov/john-lewis/biography

Drakeford, M. (1998). Last rights? Funerals, poverty, and social exclusion. *Journal of Social Policy*, 27(4), 507–524.

Eskew, G.T. (2001). From Civil War to Civil Rights. *International Journal of Hospitality & Tourism Administration*, 2(3–4), 201–214.

Francaviglia, R.V. (1971). The cemetery as an evolving cultural landscape. *Annals of the Association of American Geographers*, 61(3), 501–509.

Francis, D. (2003). Cemeteries as cultural landscapes. *Mortality*, 8(2), 222–227.

Garber, C.M. (1934). Some mortuary customs of the Western Alaska Eskimos. *The Scientific Monthly*, 39(3), 203–220.

Jamieson, R.W. (1995). Material culture and social death: African-American burial practices. *Historical Archaeology*, 29(4), 39–58.

Jelbert, W. (2018). Living next door to Russia: How the remotest US community stays happy. Retrieved from: https://medium.com/thrive-global/living-next-door-to-russia-how-the-remotest-us-community-stays-happy-ebbe0cdd1d99

Jones, D. (1999). The city of the dead: The place of cultural identity and environmental sustainability in the African-American cemetery. *Landscape Journal*, 30(2), 226–240.

King, C. (2010). Separated by death and color: The African American Cemetery of New Philadelphia, Illinois. *Historical Archaeology*, 44, 125–137.

Laurie, A. & Neimeyer, R.A. (2008). African Americans in bereavement: Grief as a function of ethnicity. *OMEGA*, 57(2), 173–193.

Long, S.O. & Buehring, S. (2014). Searching for life in death: Celebratory mortuary ritual in the context of US interfaith families. *Mortality*, 19(1), 80–100.

Longoria, T. (2014). Are we all equal at death? Death competence in municipal cemetery management. *Death Studies*, 38, 355–364.

Montero, D. (2016). A somber Orlando begins funerals in wake of Orlando shooting. Retrieved from: www.dailynews.com/2016/06/18/a-somber-orlando-begins-funerals-in-wake-of-orlando-shooting/

Municipality of Anchorage (2019). History. Retrieved from: www.muni.org/Departments/health/cemetery/Pages/history.aspx

My Jewish Learning (2019). Why do Jews put stones on graves? Retrieved from: www.myjewishlearning.com/article/ask-the-expert-stones-on-graves/

46 *Cultural Competency in Cemetery Management*

Parkes, C.M., Laungani, P., & Young, B. (2015). *Death and bereavement across cultures (2nd Edition)*. New York: Routledge.

Peeples, M. (2015). The racist history behind the iconic Selma bridge. Retrieved from: www.npr.org/sections/codeswitch/2015/03/05/391041989/the-racist-history-behind-the-iconic-selma-bridge

Peters, X. & Cavacini, S. (2019). Orlando's Greenwood Cemetery is getting a memorial to Pulse victims. Retrieved from: www.orlandoweekly.com/Blogs/archives/2019/03/11/orlandos-greenwood-cemetery-is-getting-a-memorial-to-pulse-victims

Pine, V.R. & Phillips, D.L. (1970). The cost of dying: A sociological analysis of funeral expenditures. *Social Problems*, 17(3), 405–417.

Seabrook, L. (2019). Orlando City Council approves Pulse memorial at Greenwood cemetery. Retrieved from: www.wftv.com/news/local/orlando-city-council-approves-pulse-memorial-at-greenwood-cemetery/929416244

Smith, R. (2018). At least 68 Selma city jobs on chopping block after budget oversight. Retrieved from: www.wsfa.com/2018/10/15/selma-set-layoff-dozens-city-employees/

Spies, M. (2017). A graveyard, and a caretaker, for victims of the Pulse massacre. Retrieved from: www.newyorker.com/news/news-desk/a-graveyard-and-a-caretaker-for-victims-of-the-pulse-massacre

Stanley, T. (2016). The disappearance of a distinctly black way to mourn. Retrieved from: www.theatlantic.com/business/archive/2016/01/black-funeral-homes-mourning/426807/

US Census Bureau (2019). Selma, Alabama. Retrieved from: www.census.gov/quickfacts/selmacityalabama

Walter, T. (2017). Bodies and ceremonies: is the UK funeral industry still fit for purpose?, *Mortality*, 22(3), 194–208.

Walter, T. (2015). Secularisation. In *Death and bereavement across cultures* (C.M. Parkes, P. Laungani, W. Young, eds.) London: Routledge, pp. 134–148.

Wygant, E. (2016). Out of time and out of space: Chapel Hill's cemeteries are at capacity. Retrieved from: www.dailytarheel.com/article/2016/09/out-of-time-and-out-of-space-chapel-hills-cemeteries-are-at-capacity

5 Dark Tourism and the Cemetery

> I deal with everything that a city does. It's just the people are quieter.
> (Christopher Cooke, superintendent of cemeteries, City of Evansville, Illinois)

Deadwood, South Dakota is a tourist town. Nestled in the state's Black Hills region, Deadwood is known for ushering in a gold rush in 1874 (Deadwood Chamber of Commerce, 2019). Figures such as Calamity Jane and Wild Bill Hickok called the town home and are now buried in Mount Moriah Cemetery. Bob Nelson, the city's public works director who also oversees cemetery operations, told me Mount Moriah pre-dates the city's incorporation, with some of the first burials in Deadwood traced to 1878 (City of Deadwood, 2019). The city was incorporated and platted in 1881, he explained.

Deadwood's primary source of revenue is tourism, gaming, resorts, and spas. Bob explained the entire town is a national historic landmark district since 1966, and some money earned from the booming gaming industry goes into historic preservation. "So there's a licensing fee per device or table that is placed in Deadwood," he said, and some of that money has helped a multi-million dollar renovation of historic Mount Moriah cemetery.

The cemetery has a storied history, becoming the city's first official burial space in 1878 after county commissioners realized the Whitewood Gulch area was too flat to properly secure bodies (Center for Historic Cemeteries Preservation, n.d.). Mount Moriah became the final burial place for both the city's elite and poor, with distinctive grave markers showing socio-economic standing even after death. Bob said when Mount Moriah came to be, some bodies needed to be relocated from Whitewood Gulch.

> Part of the cemetery in the very beginning was located in that neighborhood (a presidential district where all the streets are named after presidents) and then it was relocated up higher on the hill. Evidently not everyone got moved when that happened. We've had a few retaining wall projects. In fact, this was before my time, but there was a home built in the presidential district, and they found some bodies when they were

48 *Dark Tourism and the Cemetery*

putting the basement in. So, there's a very lengthy process whenever you find a body. We have a dedicated portion of the cemetery, which is on city property that's separate from Mount Moriah but it's really close, so we reinterred those people there. And we actually had a ceremony for everyone one of those.

One of those found people has an interesting story. Known as the Deadwood Pioneer today, the remains, specifically the skull, were sent to forensic anthropologist Dr. Diane France in Colorado (Taylor, 2017). Karen Taylor, a forensic portrait artist, also worked on the remains, using a detailed digital rendering technique to approximate what this person might have looked like in life. Scientists, artists, and historians worked together to determine the remains were of a white male, likely wealthier thanks to gold fillings in his teeth. The Deadwood Pioneer took about five years to identify and is now a local legend within the city (Pearson, 2017). (The article from the *Black Hills Pioneer* gives additional details on the preservation team and process, along with a story from South Dakota Public Broadcasting.)

Bob told me that Deadwood has a permanent population of about 1,200 people yet Mount Moriah attracts nearly 100,000 visitors annually, while Deadwood itself attracts about 2.2 million visitors. There is not a permanent staff to handle all the tourist traffic, and the city asks for a $2 donation to go toward maintenance. People flock to see the gravesites of the gold rush pioneers like Calamity Jane and Wild Bill Hickok. "Any given day in the cemetery you can probably hear 15 different languages," he said. A local company contracts with the city to run bus tours seven days a week, and people on those tours are not counted toward the 100,000 annual visitors so that number surely is higher, Bob said. "There's so much history from here. The gold fever time period, Custer expedition, the Black Hills. There's so much stuff it's pretty cool."

Cemetery tourism is not new, but it does sometimes take an unknown toll on the grounds, increasing costs for city administrators. This chapter details dark tourism and the ways in which some cemetery managers in this study handle the large influx of tourists to their cemeteries. Some sextons also told me about doing deliberate events and marketing to attract people to demystify the stigma surrounding cemeteries as scary places.

Dark Tourism: Our Fascination with Death

I like to tell people I had lunch with Coco Chanel. When I was attending a conference in Lausanne, Switzerland, the hotel I was staying at was outside of conference venue, so I had to take a train to the campus. Each day the train would clang along past a cemetery I could see in the distance. I knew I had to find this cemetery; it looked close enough to the train stop for a walk. When

Dark Tourism and the Cemetery   49

Photo 5.1 Coco's Grave.

the conference ended, I grabbed a sandwich from the cafeteria, packed it in my backpack, and set off on foot for the cemetery thanks to help from my GPS. I had no idea the name of the cemetery, so I simply typed cemetery into the map app and hoped for the best.

50 Dark Tourism and the Cemetery

Turns out it is named Bois-de-Vaux Cemetery, and I spent several hours wandering around the manicured green space. Each section is easily numbered, and there are information boards throughout the cemetery telling you where to locate certain notables. I found Coco Chanel's grave and decided to eat my lunch nearby. I saw other visitors milling about, enjoying a calm afternoon almost shielded from the busy street just outside the cemetery's borders.

Visiting cemeteries for me is not uncommon. It is a running joke that I will find a cemetery wherever I go. Why? I cannot explain it, really. I have an interest in history, and even if I do not know the stories of people buried in the cemetery, I tend to make it up or at least wonder what their lives were like. Gosh, this person died young; I wonder why? This stone looks fancy, what did they do in life? And it turns out I am not alone. Cemetery tourism usually falls under the dark tourism and/or heritage tourism umbrellas, as our fascination with the macabre draws us to these places where our minds can wander about the sometimes unknown.

Dark tourism within a cemetery space is an interesting mix of potential sadness with a chance to solemnly reflect on one's own life (Levitt, 2012). Some of the world's most popular tourist sites would fall into this dark tourism category – Holocaust sites throughout Europe, battle grounds, Ground Zero in New York City (Stone, 2006), and now sites of mass shootings in the US. Stone (2006) explains dark tourism is complex, driven by both supply and demand as consumers seek more opportunities to engage with the macabre. As such, there is debate about where cemeteries belong when it comes to dark tourism. Are they really dark tourism sites because most cemeteries are not built to be tourist attractions but can become such based upon notables buried within? Are cemeteries romantic, sensational, or commercial enough to be considered dark tourism?

Dark tourism does not have to be scary or depraved; instead, it is a chance to reflect on life's finality (Cohen, 2018). Take for instance the famous Pére-Lachaise Cemetery in Paris, which essentially ushered in cemetery marketing and tourism when "famous" residents were reinterred there in the 1800s (Touissant & Decrop, 2013). Dark tourism is usually motivated by what an individual wants to achieve, so visiting a cemetery becomes a mechanism to achieve pragmatic or existential ends (Touissant & Decrop, 2013). Visiting a cemetery for touristic reasons can help people achieve a sense of belonging or community, especially when visiting the markers for famous or infamous people, or events (Stone, 2009).

Thanatourism, or visiting cemetery sites, has been around for centuries, with people wanting to visit catacombs in France and Italy, and American cemeteries built like parks were natural sites people wanted to visit (Seaton, 2002). In the Victorian Era, people engaged in monument reading, epitaph collecting, and brass rubbing – all movements toward preserving what some thought was an endangered history. Thanatourism dropped during the first

Dark Tourism and the Cemetery 51

half of the 20th century because of anti-Victorian sentiment and the ravages of two world wars that pushed visitors to graves of war dead rather than civilians. Like most things, the dips are cyclic and more people want to visit sites that have, to them, a connection or out of sheer curiosity (Seaton, 2002).

Richard Gerbasi is cemeteries director in Savannah, Georgia. Savannah is a quaint, old Southern town that draws a lot of its economic impact from tourism, which supports more than 27,000 jobs and adds $2.8 billion to the local economy (City of Savannah, 2018). Gerbasi and his team manage five municipal cemeteries in Savannah: Colonial Park, Laurel Grove North, Laurel Grove South, Bonaventure, and Greenwich. His background is in construction and masonry, and when the housing market crashed around 2010, he took a job with the cemetery as a conservation technician. That was more than a decade ago, and since then he has moved up into the director position.

Savannah's cemeteries are world-renowned tourist attractions with hundreds of thousands of visitors coming each year. Historical photographs dating to the 1800s show people using some of the city's cemeteries as a passive park for leisure and picnicking. The city's Bonaventure Cemetery was the inspiration for the book *Midnight in the Garden of Good and Evil*, and the book's cover showcases a famous statue that became such a tourist icon that it was relocated to a museum. Gerbasi said:

> You've got to find that balance because of course you have people out there visiting their family or you have a funeral, then at the same time you have a van or bus or Segway, there's a golf cart. You have to find that balance between cemetery and tourist destination.

As tourism increased to Savannah's cemeteries, they created an event coordinator position to interface with the community and tour companies. He said, "when it comes to cemeteries, especially historical cemeteries or anywhere in general, it obviously has it benefits but it also leaves a footprint." He explained it was a balance, so I asked for an example. The event coordinator interfaces with tour bus companies working with groups of ten or more people to ensure some level of crowd control. Large groups or tour companies must register their events as a means for tracking some of the traffic. Before the event coordinator position, there was almost a free for all with little regulation of when groups would show up. Indeed, in the 2000s, the city updated its cemetery ordinance to better regulate tourism and tour companies. (Read the ordinance here: www.savannahga.gov/1549/Cemetery-Tourism-and-Special-Events).

A big question for Gerbasi and his team is how do you balance tourism while maintaining the cemetery's historic qualities? One answer is through strategic planning and capital investments. There is a need for more parking, and a new columbarium was set for completion at the end of 2019. He also

52 *Dark Tourism and the Cemetery*

authorized purchase of signage when funerals are taking place so visitors know to be respectful. There also is a lot of facility maintenance that needs to be done, and soon his team will shift from larger capital investments to working on rehabbing existing structures and facilities.

Tish Hopkins is the cemetery supervisor in Concord, Massachusetts. Like Richard Gerbasi in Savannah, she also oversees historically rich cemeteries. Sleepy Hollow is municipally owned and is still active for burials. Sleepy Hollow is the final resting place for prominent authors including Ralph Waldo Emerson, who gave a speech at the cemetery's dedication, Louisa May Alcott, Nathaniel Hawthorne, and Henry David Thoreau. Many of the authors rest together in an area called Authors' Ridge, and Tish said there is a lot of visitor traffic to these and other areas throughout Sleepy Hollow. "I keep maps in my truck. No matter what I'm doing I'll get stopped.... We get school buses full of people," she said.

Visiting the graves of famous authors highlights an interesting intersection between literary tourism and dark tourism (Brown, 2016). In her study, Brown (2016) found that people visited graves of Jean-Paul Sartre and Simone de Beauvoir in Paris either by accident (stumbling upon them while touring the cemetery) or to make a pilgrimage to visit people that had some influence on their lives. Many left tokens of appreciation or communed with the dead via these trinkets or personal conversations that were, of course, one way. It makes sense, then, for cemetery managers looking to make extra money or attract visitors to destigmatize perceptions of cemeteries would turn toward marketization of key figures buried within.

It is another tale of finding balance between tourist interest, historical preservation, and cemetery maintenance at Sleepy Hollow. Tish Hopkins told me the Emerson family members asked several years ago for a chain to be removed from around the family plots so the public had better access when visiting.

> We saved [the chain]. They called us last year and said can you put it back up because all the grass was dead from people standing on it. We re-lawned and seeded and put it back up. People are walking on it constantly. I've seen old pictures of the cemetery from the early 1900s with signs saying "keep off the grass." I feel like people would ignore them today, so I don't know if it would do us any good to put them back out. Thoreau's lot is just dirt.

Tish has been with the cemetery for 32 years, so she sees it as her job to take care of not only the living families but also the dead. But that sense of public service is literally in her blood. Her father worked for the town's lighting department, her uncle was a mechanic for the highway department, and a cousin worked for the highway department as well.

Dark Tourism and the Cemetery 53

Whatever was going on in our lives stopped because the Town of Concord needed my father. It didn't matter if it was Christmas and snowing, we would wait until dad got home. The Town of Concord has come first in my life since I was born. This is it. My birthday is four days after Christmas and more times we didn't have it because daddy was at work. It was okay. It was just expected.

While some cemeteries are natural attractions for tourists given historical figures or popular media attention, others actively invited people to explore the cemetery through public history events. Chris Waite, the cemetery supervisor in Billings, Montana, said throughout the summer there are heritage tours in Mountview Cemetery, which dates to 1881. The walking tours take place mostly during the summer months given the region's climate. Summer camp groups also visit during their sessions to learn about the city's history.

Megan Wimberley is the special events coordinator for the City of Bainbridge, Georgia, and part of her responsibilities include the cemetery. There are four municipally owned cemeteries in Bainbridge: Oak City, Jonas Lobe, West Bainbridge, and Pine View. Megan started in her position in 2016 and plans more than 30 events each year, including living history tours in the cemeteries, a popular bluegrass music festival, a community July 4 celebration, Halloween haunted hayrides, and Christmas events. Suffice to say, she does a lot of work.

She told me about some of the living history events inside Oak City Cemetery. These tours began in 2012 as a partnership between the city, the Convention and Visitors Bureau, and the Downtown Development Authority to attract more visitors to the cemetery. Actors, either from the local high school or community theater, will adopt personas of the deceased and bring them back to life, so to speak. Megan will travel to Oak Ridge and pick out a few names with gravesites within reasonable walking distance from each other then get to work researching about the peoples' lives. She relies on old books, historical documents, church records, obituaries and more to construct a story of how these people lived. She picks about seven people for the actors to portray, and one person learns the lines and stories of one person to depict. Each tour takes her about four months to prepare given all the research needed to find historical details and write the scripts. The living history tours attract about 400 people, with a group of 20 setting off on the tour every 15 minutes.

Bainbridge is a relatively small town, and Megan said the living history events bring out these connections further. A local actor, for example, portrayed his great- great-grandfather who is buried in the cemetery. Another person buried in Oak City lived in the former Bon Air Hotel, and a person attending the cemetery tour recognized the story, learning the person was indeed her great- great-grandmother. "It's more than just a tour through a

54 *Dark Tourism and the Cemetery*

cemetery. A lot of these people, these are your family. They find out through tours that I'm actually related to this person."

Walking tours or living history events are a perfect example of the tensions found in dark tourism – the commodification of cemetery spaces leading the way to a seemingly safe encounter with death through an historic lens. No matter the motivations, these kinds of experiences are interesting ways to showcase the history of the place and people (Venbrux, 2010). Cemetery tourism is a way to reflect on death while still seemingly being apart from it when done through an historical view or a walking tour using a guide map – we are there but not quite there yet (Blom, 2000).

The Super Bowl for Cemeteries

Living history events are popular ways sextons in this study bring people into the cemetery that does not involve a ghost tour. I took a cemetery tour with Don Price and my parents when they visited me one summer in Orlando. Don told a story about a round sphere on top of an obelisk. The ball, meant to be a cannon ball, was stolen so a local group replaced it with a bowling ball glued hole-side down. We never would know that walking through the cemetery if it were not for that anecdote. Don talked at length to my parents and I after the tour about how he got into the business, his life after retirement, and how he remains connected to Orlando through telling these stories.

Cemetery tourism for some of the sextons in my research was a Catch-22. For those working in cities with hugely popular cemeteries, like Savanah and Boston, tourism was almost a necessary evil because it can take a toll on cemetery grounds. For those in other areas, many wanted to attract visitors to the cemetery to showcase local history. As noted above, a popular way to do that is through the living history tours. Memorial Day and Veterans Day events were incredibly popular – and stressful – for some in my study.

"Memorial Day is basically what I call the Super Bowl of the cemetery," explained Bill Bibby from Charlotte, North Carolina. He said there are certain days he knows are more popular than others for visitors – Memorial Day, Veterans Day, Father's Day, Mother's Day, Easter. That means he needs to watch his budget throughout the year to ensure he has more to dedicate to maintenance and cleaning during those times of year.

Connie Goedert in Queensbury, New York hit a snag during her first Memorial Day celebration event. She said there was a mix up regarding who needed to order the flags that go on each veteran's stone. The town clerk usually had that responsibility, but that person left so the flags were not ordered. "Needless to say, I order the flags now," she said. "I have it marked on the calendar January 1 to order flags."

I asked Bob Bernhardt from the City of Logansport, Illinois, some of the favorite parts of his job. "When it's all said and done, there's a lot of favorite

Dark Tourism and the Cemetery 55

Photo 5.2 Don Price giving a cemetery tour.

parts," he said. He described the town's Memorial Day event, which includes a parade that marches to the cemetery. "I'm busy all Monday morning of Memorial Day setting this up so they can have their services," telling me there are two services in two different parts of the cemetery. He makes sure

56 *Dark Tourism and the Cemetery*

all the logistics are set, including setting up chairs, sound speakers, and other items for the ceremonies. "When it's all said and done people walk up to you and say the cemetery looks fantastic. That's a good feeling."

About 300 people annually show up to the event, Bob said. He recalls the ceremony in 2018 was special because he did not have anyone to sing the National Anthem.

> They couldn't get a band to do the National Anthem, and I was sitting in the back a little ways, and I just shouted "let's sing it." Everybody sang it. It was heart jerking. Hopefully that follows through this year, too. It was amazing. Everybody took off. They just started singing it. I'm not a speaking-type person, but I had to say that. I had to say let's sing it, so we did.

Recognizing Memorial Day in the US is akin to other ceremonies overseas including Armistice Day (Grant, 2005). Memorial Day originated as Decoration Day to honor the Civil War dead in the US (Grant, 2005). Many of the practices sextons in this research described have roots in historical celebrations – parades, celebrations of the deceased, cemetery decorations. The cemetery itself became the center of pomp and circumstance surrounding Memorial Day, which explains why so many of the sextons interviewed wanted the events to be perfect because they are reflections of them, the city, and the cemetery. Grant (2005) deftly details how Northerners and Southerners commemorated the day differently, but Memorial Day has come to symbolize America's fascination with nation building and rugged individualism.

The big events and walking tours are special occasions where people come visit the cemetery. Sometimes living history tours also could include battle reenactments to build camaraderie and community (Hartmann, 2014). Apart from that, cemeteries are traditionally public parks where people can spend free time – for good or ill. A couple sextons told me there have been fights between people in the cemetery, drug use and deals, and even wild animals roaming through. (Dawn Ubelaker in Nome, Alaska said bears are common visitors to her city cemetery.) For the most part, though, the cemeteries are peaceful places that are at once active and passive – bustling with visitors, workers, and mourners, and quiet with the deceased.

Like others, Bender (1974) traces this cemeteries-as-public-places movement to the rural cemetery transformation, whereby cemeteries were moved from city centers to the outskirts and designed akin to English landscapes. "America's rural cemeteries were explicitly designed for both the living and for the dead, and the assumptions underlying their widespread popularity were central to mid-nineteenth-century American ideas about the relation of cityscape and landscape in urbanizing society" (Bender, 1974, pp. 196–197).

Conversely, a more critical look at cemetery design and landscape could see how the physical spaces were a manifestation of Foucauldian control of the body even in death (Johnson, 2008). Cemeteries started as places to dispose of bodies that could bring disease to cities, so the cemetery became a place to contain potential sickness. But as geometry and math came into grid

Photo 5.3 Bangor Cemetery Flags.
Source: Photo courtesy Neal Currie, Bangor, Maine.

58 *Dark Tourism and the Cemetery*

once-haphazard burial spaces, those means became ways to control bodies further (Johnson, 2008). For Foucault, rank was a way to control bodies, and this was seen in the kinds of markers placed on graves, given those with higher status and social rank often could physically wall off family plots and/or install large markers to showcase their family grandeur even in death.

Despite changing mourning practices, and shifting cemetery design, the cemetery remains a place in constant tension. As Sloane (2018) details, many of today's memorial practices find roots in the historic past. There was movement to relocate death from the family unit to the more corporatized hospital and funeral home settings, and now there is a shift back to public memorials via online spaces, roadside monuments, or commemorative monuments (like the Vietnam Veterans Memorial in Washington, DC or the traveling AIDS Memorial Quilt). One needs to distinguish, though, between memorials inside a cemetery versus outside. Inside, cemetery ordinances dictate what kinds of items can be placed on graves, and even what kinds of grave markers to use. Outside, where there are no formal rules or norms, one can be freer with memorial markers that bring death into public life in a sometimes-jarring manner. People expect to confront death in a cemetery, while it might be unexpected when a new roadside memorial pops up (Sloane, 2018).

Neal Currie from Bangor, Maine explained the Memorial Day ceremony in his city is a connection to the past. Like the other sextons, Neal said Memorial Day is a large community gathering, and Neal and his crew, along with local special needs high school student volunteers, put out more than 3,000 flags on veterans' graves. He said at least two weeks before, he will work with the mowing contractors to make sure the cemetery looks its best. "People take the cemetery plots as sacred ground, and if there's something wrong they call me up." Hundreds of people attend the event, and Neal makes sure to have records available for those wanting to genealogical research. Records in Bangor are not online because of privacy concerns, he said, so people can look through burial books to see causes of death for relatives. "Some of these people are quite shocked what their relatives died of. It makes people interested in the cemetery."

Concluding Remarks

All told, the cemetery managers needed to find a balance between historic preservation, tourism, and maintenance. It is a tricky line to cross, especially as many sextons want to remove the stigma surrounding cemeteries as foreboding places. For me, I find it interesting that people are afraid to cemeteries yet at Halloween time willingly decorate their houses with makeshift graveyards and skeletons. Somehow those decorations are less terrifying than the real thing.

Dark tourism is a contested scholarly topic, with debates about what really counts as part of this umbrella term. Stone (2006) offers a dark tourism spectrum, with the darkest tourism taking someone directly to sites of death and

Photo 5.4 Halloween Grave.

suffering on one end, and on the other is the lightest form of dark tourism at sites associated with death and suffering. He gives an example that a Holocaust museum is associated with death, while the concentration camps are the sites of death. A cemetery might not purposefully be constructed as a tourist site but becomes one when people make trips to visit famous people buried inside. The purpose of these trips could be to learn about figures, make pilgrimages to see celebrities, or reconcile guilt of past actions (Ashworth & Isaac, 2015).

Returning to Bob Nelson from Deadwood, he said people come to the city's cemetery to connect with the past, to learn more about the figures from the gold rush era. Given there is so much foot traffic, through the years the city has made improvements, including installing an asphalt trail with gravel on top so it blends more into the landscape. There is not much marketing or advertising – the tourism happens naturally. Though the Deadwood Historic Preservation Commission has its own YouTube channel and features some cemetery-related stories. At Mount Moriah, "we actually have a little bit of an interpretive museum" and there is a $2 charge, in place before the gaming sprung up, and that money goes back to cemetery preservation.

This is what I mean by thanatourism as a Catch-22 – how do you keep cemeteries open and public while also maintaining them to the level people

60 *Dark Tourism and the Cemetery*

expect? The sextons interviewed for this research each had mechanisms for coping with that stress – event coordinator, strategic planning, signs to keep off the grass, tour company regulations. At the end of the day, though, cemeteries are historically public places for gathering, and the sextons intend to keep them that way no matter the circumstances.

References

Ashworth, G.J. & Isaac, R.K. (2015). Have we illuminated the dark? Shifting perspectives on "dark" tourism. *Tourism Recreation Research*, 40(3), 316–325.

Bender, T. (1974). The "rural" cemetery movement: Urban travail and the appeal of nature. *The New England Quarterly*, 47(2), 196–211.

Blom, T. (2000). Morbid tourism – a postmodern market niche with an example from Althorp. *Norsk Geografisk Tidsskrift*, 54(1), 29–36.

Brown, L. (2016). Tourism and pilgrimage: Paying homage to literary heroes. *International Journal of Tourism Research*, 18, 167–175.

Center for Historic Cemeteries Preservation (n.d.). Mt. Moriah historical overview. Retrieved from: www.cityofdeadwood.com/vertical/sites/%7BECDE07BE-19F7–4F11-A017-CFDAD3EEEE69%7D/uploads/Mt_Moriah_Cemetery_Historical_Overview.pdf

City of Deadwood (2019). Mount Moriah Cemetery. Retrieved from: www.cityofdeadwood.com/?SEC=A0DB4AD3-F0E9–4EAC-8E22–995D27A3329B

City of Savannah (2018). Savannah tourism management plan. Retrieved from: www.savannahga.gov/DocumentCenter/View/14245/Tourism-Management-Plan?bidId=

Cohen, E. (2018). Thanatourism: A comparative approach. In *The Palgrave Handbook of Dark Tourism Studies* (P.R. Stone et al., eds.). New York: Palgrave Macmillan, pp. 157–172.

Deadwood Chamber of Commerce (2019). History. Retrieved from: www.deadwood.com/history/

Grant, S. (2005). Raising the dead: War, memory, and American national identity. *Nations and Nationalism*, 11(4), 509–529.

Hartmann, R. (2014). Dark tourism, thanatourism, and dissonance heritage tourism management: New directions in contemporary tourism research. *Journal of Heritage Tourism*, 9(2), 166–182.

Johnson, P. (2008). The modern cemetery: A design for life. *Social & Cultural Geography*, 9(7), 777–790.

Levitt, L. (2012). Solemnity and celebration: Dark tourism experiences at Hollywood Forever cemetery. *Journal of Unconventional Parks, Tourism & Recreation Research*, 4(1), 20–25.

Pearson, J.C. (2017). Meet the Deadwood pioneer. Retrieved from: www.bhpioneer.com/deadwood/meet-the-deadwood-pioneer/article_823ef9ea-3b0e-11e7-ad19-efc8200300ce.html

Seaton, A.V. (2002). Thanatourism's final frontiers? Visits to cemeteries, churchyards, and funerary sites as sacred and secular pilgrimage. *Tourism Recreation Research*, 27(2), 73–82.

Sloane, D.C. (2018). *Is the cemetery dead?* Chicago: University of Chicago Press.

Stone, P.R. (2009). Dark tourism: Morality and new moral spaces. In *The darker side of travel* (R. Sharpley & P.R. Stone, eds.). United Kingdom: Channel View Publications, pp. 56–74.

Stone, P.R. (2006). A dark tourism spectrum: Towards a typology of death and macabre related tourist sites, attractions, and exhibitions. *Tourism: An International Interdisciplinary Journal*, 54(2), 145–160.

Taylor, K.T. (2017). Historical project – Deadwood Pioneer. Retrieved from: www.behance.net/gallery/53679421/Historical-Project-Deadwood-Pioneer

Touissant, S. & Decrop, A. (2013). The Pere-Lachaise Cemetery: Between dark tourism and heterotopic consumption. In *Dark tourism and place identity* (L. White & E. Frew, eds.). London: Routledge, pp. 13–25.

Venbrux, E. (2010). Cemetery tourism: Coming to terms with death? *La Ricerca Folklorica*, 61, 41–49.

6   Empathy and Beyond

I just say it's caring. We actually care about the people we see all the time and that you help. It's the care. It's not, it's not a hostile world. Nothing's hostile at the time. You don't have to worry about anything. You're there because you're helping them.

(Connie Goedert, cemetery superintendent, Town of Queensbury, New York)

With cemetery sextons, we are seeing people at their worst. A lot of times we're meeting with families that just lost a loved one. We're looking at buying cemetery lots, and it's one of those decisions where it's a decision that you have to make right now because the funeral is tomorrow but it's a decision you've got to live with from now on. Once we put somebody in the ground, they're there. It's not like buying a house and five years from now you say hey I want to move over there.

Terrell Stallings told me that story during our conversation. Terrell is the sexton in the City of Dalton, Georgia. Dalton is in the northwest part of the state near the Blue Ridge Mountains. Terrell became sexton in 2014 when the person in the position stepped down. Before moving to the cemetery to fill in for the prior sexton, Terrell worked in parks and recreation overseeing maintenance in various recreation spots throughout the city. He moved over to public works to hopefully get a calmer schedule then took over cemetery operations a few years later.

West Hill Cemetery is the largest city-owned cemetery in Dalton at about 70 acres. Funeral homes in the area dig the graves, so Terrell oversees daily operations, maintenance, records, and much more. When he first took the job, "I thought it was going to be easier at first, but now it's gotten to that point where it's not too bad." He said the biggest learning curve was familiarizing himself with all the cemetery rules, regulations, and policies. The city also owns two older cemeteries, but there are no active burials in those. He said:

As a cemetery sexton you have to be a receptionist, secretary, treasurer, a manager, architect. I mean and the list just goes on and on and on. I'm kind of in a special situation. I'm part of Public Works, but I'm almost kind of a standalone, and I sort of do my own thing. Yes, I answer to City Hall, but as far as Public Works goes, I don't have anything to do with Public Works. That's really good. Then the other thing here, nobody wants anything to do with the cemetery. Nobody wants the headache of the cemetery. It's nothing but complaints. In a normal situation you're trying to make one customer happy. In the cemetery business, I mean, I have like I said 26,000 people buried over there. You look at that as 26,000 families you're trying to keep happy every day. Because that family that comes once a year to see their loved ones, everything is supposed to be perfect on their lot when they left it. Families come over there, and they look at their lots. That's it. They're not looking at the whole picture. And that's where as a cemetery sexton we have to look at the whole picture, but we also have to keep those individuals, look at it as individual pictures.

Terrell told me that helping families is "almost like a gift" and not something you necessarily learn. This theme kept popping up during data analysis, and I struggled with thinking through how public servants deal with death each day. Perhaps it is empathy? Perhaps it is servant leadership? Perhaps it is public service motivation? Perhaps it is something new?

Empathy is understanding and responding to feelings of other people (Edlins & Dolamore, 2018). Edlins and Dolamore (2018) explain empathy is often viewed as a pro-social, desirable behavior of public servants. Empathy is not easy to understand given there are active and passive definitions, and through a conceptual analysis Wiseman (1996) distills four aspects of empathy: (1) see the world as others see it; (2) non-judgmental; (3) understanding another's feelings; and (4) communicate that understanding.

Sextons in this research seemed to exhibit all four of Wiseman's (1996) empathetic aspects. Regarding the first, seeing the world as others see it, some cemetery managers said they felt more connected to people when they have experienced loss themselves. Melissa Haynes of Ruidoso, New Mexico said she lost her mother, aunt, two uncles and her husband's grandmother in the span of four months in 2019.

> Going through what I just went through with my mom I think it's given me a whole other level of that of, like, understanding and knowing what they're going through ... I mean, I can handle just about anything at this point.

Being non-judgmental involves learning about other cultures, helping people in a time of need, and providing information rather than selling extra

64　*Empathy and Beyond*

items. Chapter 4 details the role of cultural competency in cemetery management and the associated social justice issues therein. Understanding another's feelings is clearly a big part of the job and communicating that goes hand in hand with cemetery management. Many of the stories in this chapter touch on both these vital aspects of being a sexton. As Ken Carroll, the sexton from the Plainfield Township cemetery in Plainfield, Illinois, said, "You don't walk up to people when you know they're coming to you for the worst thing in the world. I keep it light out here. You don't ever ask someone how you're doing out there."

It seems many of the cemetery managers display empathy but on the deeper level Guy and Mastracci (2018) indicate. They seemingly exhibit empathy not only in interactions with families directly but also with historical grave makers, when maintaining the cemetery, when enforcing policies. Many take the jobs home with them as well. I arrange the stories here into three categories: (1) interacting with families; (2) taking the job home; and (3) learning as you go.

How public servants in cemeteries interact with families ties into how people feel about and emotionally connect with government. These exchanges involve feelings, mutuality, exchange, and cannot be captured on a spreadsheet (Guy, 2019). This chapter highlights the lived experiences of the public servants dealing with death – something we often do not think about as a municipal good.

What all the stories below show is extensive emotional labor, understood as the ways in which employees try to engage in organizationally and socially acceptable behaviors when at work (Hsieh, Yang, & Fu, 2011). Emotional labor usually involves two key aspects: emotional regulation, and surface and deep acting. Surface acting involves managing expressing emotions, while deep acting is how one manages the actual emotions (Grandey, 2000; Hsieh et al., 2011). As a result of constant emotional labor, burnout could occur (Grandey, 2000).

Interacting with Families

> I used to be so scared of death. I didn't want to talk about it. The first year, death creeped me out. Now I respect it and know that it's coming. It's weird, but it's like I'm at peace with it, whereas when I first took the job I wasn't. I think that's just the lack of maturity I had.

Those words came from Christopher Cooke, the superintendent of cemeteries in the City of Evansville, Indiana. There are two municipal cemeteries, Locust Hill and Oak Hill Cemetery and Arboretum. There are approximately 100,000 interments between the two properties, so "that's two cities of the dead I essentially have to run." Christopher has deep connections to the city and the

Empathy and Beyond 65

cemetery. "Literally I can see my family lot from my desk that I am sitting at right now." I asked if he had any concerns before taking the superintendent job, and he told me, "I said as long as I don't start talking to dead great grandparents I've never met, we're good."

While Christopher has countless industry certifications and is a sought-after expert, he really began to understand the grief process through personal loss. When his dad died, he was able to integrate the rational and emotional sides of his brain – his empathy with expertise.

> I realized through that process of trying to get better at work, I realized how I was still struggling. Through my own experience, it really started to click when I realized what I was dealing with and how to move forward with it.

In his job, he developed "what I call a sixth sense thing" where he knows if people need his help. "When I drive by and see how they're standing at the gravesite, I can usually tell if they need me to stop and ask how they're doing. It's taken me 11 years to get to that point." He told me a story of a woman who lost her husband who would regularly change flowers on his grave. One day, she stopped into Christopher's office, explaining she was ready to die. "I looked at her and she said nobody is going to take care of her grave when she dies, and that saddens her." At that point, Christopher walked her to the office windows and told her, "I can give you my word that I can walk my big ass from my family's spot to pay some respects to your family's spot when I'm out here paying respects to my family. That took a gut instinct."

Understanding how the sextons in my research help and react to families addresses Guy and Mastracci's (2018) affective necessity of public servants. As they explain (2018, p. 284):

> Officials must sense the emotive state of the citizen, analyze what the desired state should be in order to have a successful encounter, determine what actions to take in order to achieve the desired state, and then modify their own behavior in order to achieve this. This instantaneous sensing and responding is emotional labor and contributes to how the citizen "feels" during the encounter and how the citizen rates the encounter afterward.

Public servants are always in a delicate balance when it comes to the public encounter. They have to balance what they see in the moment with prevailing rules and regulations. This is what makes discretion so interesting to observe and study – and sometimes frustrating to observe and study. If the encounter goes well, people might feel connected to their government or at least to the public servant. If the encounter goes poorly, people might

66 *Empathy and Beyond*

distrust government and its associated actors (Guy & Mastracci, 2018). More research, then, is needed on these public encounters.

For Debra Lane from Chapel Hill, she told me she has learned how to "put up a wall to where I could not show emotions." As the cemetery manager, she attends a lot of the funerals but "I still keep my composure because I still have my job to do." Her reflection highlights the tension of emotional labor – she told me there are times she wants to cry (and does) but at the end of the day she needs to suppress emotions to remain a stoic public servant.

Debra said a big part of her job when interacting with families is listening to their needs and delivering the best services she can under tight budget constraints.

> I always had that experience in helping people. My faith had a lot to do with that, too. I know that their soul is somewhere better but just being there and listening to what they have to say about their loved ones, just listening not saying anything. I can only give so much comfort because I work for a municipality, so I have to watch what I say. It's just sad, but my belief is it's still a celebration, but I can see they're missing a loved one that is not here with us in body anymore.

Connie Goedert, cemetery superintendent in Queensbury, New York, told me helping families is the best part of her job. Explaining the cemetery and its rules is something she sees as a way to help families through the grieving process – and finding the perfect spot for loved ones. If someone wants their loved one buried near a tree, then she will take them to available plots where that can happen. She also knows when to use her discretion to bend some rules, especially if people are grieving the loss of a child.

> We have a lot of tchotchke stuff in one section, and it's because there's a lot of young children up there. You know what, I am just glad I am not in their shoes, and we will work with them for them to keep doing what they're doing.

Which means knowing when to be a bit looser with some regulations regarding what can be on a gravesite.

She explained empathy and her role as superintendent thusly:

> My phone rings, I give everybody my cell phone number, and I tell everybody, I say there's no clock at my house. If you need something and you need to talk to me, you call me. First of all, it doesn't matter that I'm asleep because I'm going to be more awake if something happens, and I could have helped you, you know? And I've always been that way. My husband's that way. If everybody could be just nicer to everybody.

Empathy and Beyond   67

Think about it, a school bus driver is the first person to see a kid sometimes in their day. If they give them a hard time, it continues on. If that school bus drive is smart enough to say to that kid, "Hey, how are you today?" or "Hey, have a great day" or "Hey, I'll see you this afternoon," acknowledge to that kid that they're important to that kid's life. It's because we're too busy. We're going 90 miles an hour, and we haven't learned to stop and breathe.

Taking the Job Home

Don Price, the retired City of Orlando sexton, came to be known as the keeper of the dead. Families knew Don would take care of them at Greenwood Cemetery. In his more than 30 years of service, he buried babies, Pulse shooting victims, and everyone in between. "You get to that point where it's the most beautiful job in the world because when you go home at night you can go 'I made a difference.'"

He likes to say that everyone dies twice – physically then again when people stop telling your story. He referenced the popular Disney animated film *Coco*, which features a Day of the Dead theme. Family photos in the movie started to fade as the older grandmother character lost her memory and could no longer share family lore. He said:

> As long as we can tell your story you keep living ... Even when you get to the point where you mark the grave, you dig the grave, you get everything prepared so that when you show up that everything is perfect, to the point that I even had my staff make sure that the bushes were perfect when [the family] walked in that the walkway. I will ask them to walk that path. When they walk that path, I wanted everything to be perfect and I wanted everything so that when you walked up and that was your last thought that everything was great. It's taxing, it really is. But I loved every minute of it. I did.

When he retired, Don was admittedly lost. The cemetery was such a part of him:

> and I lost that identity and all I wanted was a hug, if that makes sense. I just wanted someone to come up and go, "You know what, you needed that companionship" or that someone to go, "You know what? It's okay, it's gonna be okay."

During the time he left the cemetery, Don was on a local top ten list of Orlando standout people yet felt lost. To continue with self-care and healing, Don sought therapy and the correct mix of medication.

68   *Empathy and Beyond*

> I literally lived for months on antidepressants and Xanax, I did. Of course, now I'm off, but I did. I couldn't focus on life, and that's when I even tried to take my life because I could not handle the pain and your pain when you walked in. I couldn't handle everybody's pain when they walked in.

He credits his doctor with saving his life, with listening to his concerns to ensure he was on the right path toward health.

> I mean, I was burying 15 people a week. Imagine dealing with 15 deaths a week and her going, "Get your head out of your ass. Let me take the edge off, but I'm not going to take the edge off forever. You're gonna work your ass through this." I didn't handle it great, I really didn't. Some people will tell you that they can handle it perfectly, but when they do that they're not dealing with the families, they're dealing with the job. I can tell you right now, if you come to me and you are trying to bury this or that, I take that emotion home and that's part of life. When you lose that, it's time to quit.

In my data analysis, I found mixed responses when coding for what I called taking the job home. Some managers were adamant about firmly separating work from home life, while others like Don internalized the job. Thus is the paradox of the sexton's job – they need to be empathetic, employ emotional labor and emotional intelligence, and provide a service in a professional manner to people flush with grief. To me, this seems to push beyond empathy as a passive approach; rather, empathy for sextons must be active, knowing what people need in their worst times. Active empathy goes beyond "putting yourself in someone else's shoes," so that means empathy is a constant task rather than something to be turned on and off (Edlins & Dolamore, 2018).

Sextons exhibit both cognitive and emotional empathy, the former involves adopting another's point of view, while the latter involves feelings of sympathy based on the cognitive processing. Sextons discussed the importance of reading a room. Some families might be solemn and serene, while others might come in laughing. The active empathy means sextons dealing with families need to adapt to those feelings while perhaps hiding their own. This hiding, though, was not universal as several internalized the feelings and job.

Tricia Neal from Somerset, Kentucky is someone else who internalizes grief.

> I think people can have empathy easily, and I think some people can't. I think it's definitely helpful in this job if you can be that way, and I always have been. I cry at the drop of the hat. I don't say any of that to brag because it's actually a bit of a curse to be able to feel other peoples'

Empathy and Beyond 69

pain. I've been the person who kind of feels for the other person a lot, who tries to understand what they're going through. That part did not come hard for me. I wish I didn't have to do it, but unfortunately it's part of this job.

Somerset is a small town where most everyone knows each other. Before coming to the cemetery, Tricia was a reporter and that meant covering stories about children who died.

You've got to put down the pen for a minute and cry with mom. That probably helped prepare me for this [at the cemetery]. That's just in my personality. If you come in and you've got tears in your eyes, I'm going to grab you and hug you. I'll listen until as long as you feel better. In the time that I have worked here I have lost two grandparents and a parent myself. And those were the people who were the closest to me so that gave me a really big dose of being on the other side of the table and going through this. I think that helped me even more. Losing a parent is like, I mean you do not understand it until you've been through it, and then it's like you're part of this club you didn't want to be a part of. Everybody else is like, "You get it now, don't you?" It's probably the same if you've lost a child or lost a spouse. When it's somebody that close to you, you don't get it until you've been through it.

Neal Currie, the sexton in Bangor, Maine, is on the flip side, trying to find a line between work and home. He has been sexton for 16 years and each day is still a learning experience when it comes to managing the cemeteries, of which there are four in the city: Pine Grove, Oak Grove, Maple Grove, and a section of Mount Hope. Before working for the city in public works on the paving crew, Neal served in the Army so is a lifelong public servant. When the cemetery position came open, he applied. "I was looking for a real quiet job. I'd seen enough other stuff." With the cemetery, "part of me was thinking wow that's pretty quiet out there" but about four months in "I was thinking there's a lot of hostile people out there."

For Neal, he said one thing he can never lose is his sense of humor when dealing with grief and death almost daily. He named other public service positions like police and fire who also deal with grim happenings and need to find coping mechanisms.

You've got to be able to still laugh at life, you know? You can't bring this home. You can't have your job 24/7. I try to do that when I leave work. I don't bring it home with me. Everybody's job, people do not realize until they're in that position that it can be stressful. If you can't do a job, you're going to get yourself out of it eventually because you

70   *Empathy and Beyond*

say this just isn't for me. I like dealing with patrons of the cemetery. I really like helping people. That's my main goal is to help people. Helping people helps me.

He told me several stories related to taking the extra step to help people. One is about an elderly woman who visits a cemetery five days a week to visit her husband who passed away 26 years ago. Neal sees her each time and has gotten to know her, so if she reports a shrub that needs trimming or a sunken headstone "you jump on it right away and help her."

Another instance concerns at 16-year-old high school girl killed in a car accident. Many of her classmates showed up to the service and covered the upright monument with teddy bears, butterflies, and other notes. While this was not in line with the cemetery rules and regulations, Neal made sure to bend the rules and left the items there for nearly seven months before removing them slowly. "Nobody called me on it. The high school students eventually stopped going to the grave. You've got to work with people. You can't go into this heavy handed."

Neal reminded me that cemetery sextons are a different breed, sometimes "it's a forgotten thing" because people take the cemetery work for granted. He said there is no formal schooling to be a sexton given all the myriad responsibilities involved with the job. (While you can go to school for mortuary science, the focus is largely on managing the body and land rather than managing the living.) And almost in contrast to his proclamation about not taking the job home, he said,

It's one of those positions that you worry about it. I don't know about you, but a lot of people when they clock out, they go home they don't think about work until they come back. As a cemetery sexton, you're constantly thinking about it – at night, at home on the weekend, everything. I had services over the weekend. I'm looking at my watch thinking diggings, procession, they should be about done. It's one of those things where you never stop thinking about it. I live less than five minutes from work. Ten, 11 o'clock at night, I'm getting ready for bed and think, "Did I mark that on the right-hand side or left-hand side?" and I will drive over at 11:30 to check it. It takes a special person to do what we do, and I truly believe that. When it's 11:30 at night, and I'm getting dressed and my wife is saying, "Where are you going?" I say, "I have to check it." I'm not going to sleep at all until I know this is right, until I go back over there and check this I'm not going to rest.

Craig Hudson is the cemetery manager in Auburn, Washington, a suburb of Seattle. From the cemetery, one can see Mt. Rainier, and Craig called the cemetery a "beautiful property" with different kinds of open spaces that

Empathy and Beyond 71

appeal to many seeking something relaxing and tranquil. Like some of his counterparts, Craig also worked in a private funeral home before transitioning to public service. The funeral home hours meant being constantly on call, sometimes being on an emergency at two in the morning only to return to normal working hours at nine the same day.

He sees his role as guiding families through a tough process, sometimes recommending the right resources for them be it mental support or other caretakers.

> I go to the gym every morning, and I think that definitely helps with some of that release. I do a lot of hiking on the weekends and things like that. I think it's important to be able to leave it at the office and not bring it home. I'm sure my wife has a sense of some of those days that have been a little harder than others, but she's been understanding.

To be sure, this separation is an internal tension for the sextons. It is sometimes easier said than done to not take work home. Chris Parayno is the director of cemeteries and trees in Fall River, Massachusetts and is 28 years old. He started in the position in 2018 and was still learning many of the ropes when we talked. Oak Grove is the main cemetery dating to 1855. He said it was laid out like a park so has meandering walkways and plenty of greenery.

He told me his biggest learning curve was learning how to help families coming to the cemetery.

> In this position you are literally dealing with people on the worst day of their lives. I have people come in here the day their loved one died to purchase a plot. You can see how sad and depressed they are. You have to really be friendly and be on your game and not take what is going on in your personal life when you come to work.

He said he is still learning what to say and what not to say, reading the room to understand how the family wants to grieve.

> A lot of times the families open up and talk about their loved one. It helps them in their grieving process I'm sure. It's interesting to hear some of the life stories of the people we're interring. I guess the ones that really strike home for me are when we bury younger people. I mean, I'm 28 so there's time where I'm burying people younger than me or right around my age. Life is really fragile. It's given me a lot of perspective on life, too. Those are the kinds of stories that stick out to me the most.

When Chris started, a groundskeeper gave him advice to imagine you are burying an empty box, but that becomes difficult when he gets to know the

72   *Empathy and Beyond*

families well. He tries to disconnect from work when he goes home, spending time with his family or relaxing in other ways.

> It really depends on the circumstances. The younger people we bury definitely hit home for me. When you bury someone who is 94, you kind of expect to bury someone at 94. When you bury someone in their 20s or 30s it definitely hits home a bit.

Like Chris, Melissa Haynes from Ruidoso, New Mexico also found helping families to be both the most challenging yet most rewarding part of her job. Melissa is the parks and recreation administrative assistant and taking care of the cemetery is under her purview. She said Ruidoso is a popular tourist town, attracting about 30,000 visitors on a busy weekend to the ski resorts in town. The one funeral home in Ruidoso handles not only that city but surrounding areas as well, so they are kept quite busy. Ruidoso has two city-owned cemeteries – Forest Lawn and Gavilan Memorial Gardens, which opened in 2014. Melissa has been in her job six years and is still learning the lingo.

> The funeral home director here said it's not ashes, it's cremains. It's not a hole, it's a plot. You're not digging a hole, you're opening the grave. There's certain language I was not in touch with that I'm trying to learn.

For her, there is a difference between helping an elderly couple take care of burial pre-needs versus a young family in mourning. She told me a story of a young man who came to her office after his wife died during childbirth.

> He is balling at my table in my office. I'm balling with him because I've read about her death in the newspaper. Or I know the people I just went to the cemetery to meet because their son just graduated with me son. I cry. I have goosebumps right this second. I call my husband, and I'm balling. I didn't know that was going to be part of my job, and it's become more of my job since I've worked here.

Burying babies or younger people is the toughest part of the job for the sextons to whom I spoke. Scholarship indicates people, especially mothers, mourning the death of an infant are often silenced, both physically and emotionally (Lauterbach, 2003). Lauterbach (2003) calls this phenomenological silence, meaning there is a lack of social awareness surrounding infant death, which then causes silence from the mourners and those surrounding them. This silence often spills over into healthcare and death care industries, as those trained professionals sometimes follow rules and procedures while unsure how to handle the emotional aspects of infant death.

Sometimes cemeteries have dedicated spaces to infant burials called "babyland." Through time, how people have memorialized children has changed, with parents sometimes choosing plain grave markers and others choosing something more playful and elaborate (Haveman, 1999). The death of a child or young person often is more difficult to process because it is not a part of a natural life cycle (Edgette, 1999).

Bob Bernhardt from Logansport, Indiana, said since he began as sexton in 2014, the city has added two areas called "baby walks" into Mount Hope Cemetery. The areas are peaceful, decorated, and well maintained. "So when we have an infant pass away and the family decided to go to the baby walk, that grave is free with a very minimal interment fee. Those are the hard ones."

Neal Currie from Bangor, Maine, expressed similar difficulty with burying small children. At his cemetery in the city, the funeral homes do most of the grave digging, which usually gives him a bit of a buffer when families are mourning. Though he gets the most joy from helping families,

> It's got to where now you almost, and I hate to say this, but you almost get numb to it. One of the things that still gets to me, and one of the things I dislike about this job, is when we have to bury babies. It's tough. A lot of our baby graves, we don't contract that out as far as having the funeral homes dig them. I'll do those myself because they're small. That puts me there with the family, and that's tough.

Ciera McClain oversees cemetery operations for Killeen, Texas. Killeen is a military town, and she said much of their population is transient because people are stationed in and out constantly. She grew up in Killeen so feels a personal connection to the people, the city, and cemetery. She said, "I'm the easy part of the process" because families usually deal with funeral homes in their times of immediate grief. She saw the position open and applied because "at the time for me it was mostly about the pay raise. Since I've come out here, I do have a passion for it that I didn't think I had before." When we spoke, she was two years into her role and is the first person to have that position, which the city created so there always would be an office person available to help with the financial side of the business, to take the burden off residents.

While she likes helping people the most,

> If I hold on to that it can be a little sad. I try to disconnect from it once I leave here, so maybe it's the crazy stuff that sticks in your mind. When I leave the office, I try to leave the office. I don't think about this stuff once I go home. I try my best to just turn it off. When I'm here I'm present, and when I go home, I try not to think about all the sadness of the day.

Learning as You Go

Bill Bibby, the sexton in Charlotte, North Carolina, started his cemetery career thanks to coaching youth baseball.

> I was coaching baseball and another sexton came to me and basically asked me. He noticed I took a lot of time with kids on the field. I wasn't one of those crazy screaming coaches. He'd seen empathy in me, which I never knew, and it took me into this business. I said absolutely no. It took him three times, and the third time he said, "At least can I buy you lunch?" I said okay. Then oh my God, the lights all went on.

He worked first for a private company he called the largest in the death care industry, where he learned the ropes. He came to Charlotte in 2015, and "the municipal side is totally different from the private sector. It's 180 degrees." A big difference is the financial aspect. Private cemeteries of course want to make a profit whereas municipal cemeteries are often a losing proposition, and the city takes on that maintenance responsibility especially when perpetual care is involved.

> People would walk in our office, and they would go "Do you guys sell headstones or makers?" And we go no, here's a list of people you can call. We're losing out on a lot of potential money, but on the city side of it they don't want to burn bridges with other companies so it's kind of standard procedure.

As leader, Bill and his team maintain seven cemeteries, which are basically public parks, he said. While there are people to do maintenance and records, one thing he is working on is training his crew regarding empathy.

> My crew at the city has never been trained on handling a family for a death. They are more administrative people, which I'm trying to train them now. Not to teach empathy but to think about empathy. You have to get it on their minds.

When doing job interviews, Bill sometimes asks people what they would do if a person took a bouquet of flowers and threw it in their face. He would watch how the person reacted and wait for their answer. The correct answer: stand there and take it. "I've had that happen to me. That's why I ask the question." The woman who threw the flowers was the mother whose son was killed in the recent Iraq war. "She threw flowers at me. That lady became one of my best friends."

Empathy and Beyond 75

He continued explaining to me his job involves empathy, pride, and honor.

> I think, and the way I put things is yes, we do have one shot at doing it right. The way I usually put it, and that's where sometimes like the funeral director and the cemetery won't get along very well at times, but I put it this way to the funeral director: you have them for a day and a half, I have them forever. And I think in the back of your mind, you're going to have this family forever. It doesn't happen often where you pull people out of the ground, and that's probably with empathy. Pride, you got one shot at it. The honor, you know, as a person that they may get mad at you because you're taking their loved one away. Then a few days later they understand. Those people actually chase us down to give us a hug.

Like Bill, Rob Jones in Anchorage, Alaska started his cemetery journey also via coaching. Through college, Rob cooked professionally and pursued that as a career. Then his father-in-law became ill, so one of their daughters went to daycare while Rob and his wife worked. The daycare provider's husband managed a local funeral home, so they became friends. When his father-in-law died, the funeral home sponsored Rob's then-ten-year-old son's soccer team. "We thought it was funny a funeral home would sponsor a soccer team. I was just glad to have a sponsor."

His friend who owned the funeral home saw Rob interacting with the kids and families – especially those sometimes-hyper soccer parents. "Through that, he thought that I would be a good fit as a funeral director, the way I talked to people and handled lots of different things." Like Bill, Rob took a lot of convincing before deciding to jump into the funeral industry. He eventually accepted the position with the private funeral home.

> Stupid me I thought it would be cool to wear a suit and get a pager. I quickly realized the pager goes off at 3 o'clock in the morning and you just went to bed because you had a hockey game or something.

He admittedly knew nothing about the business at first. His first surprise was just how involved the funeral homes and directors are with picking up bodies. He said during his time as a funeral director, he went to hospitals, crime scenes, car accidents, suicides, and more to help pick up bodies. This meant he was always on call, spending time away from his family.

> We would hire people who had good intentions and wanted to help and be helpful, but their first experience with a deceased individual was more than they bargained for. It's very rewarding, and it's hard to tell people that and measure that because it's a real personal thing.

76   *Empathy and Beyond*

Rob told me Anchorage is a small town, especially when it comes to the funeral business. There are six funeral homes owned by three companies, so he knew his counterparts in the public and private sectors well. When the city sexton was going to retire, he reached out to Rob to gauge his interest in the position. Rob went on the interview then got the job offer from the mayor – but the sexton decided not to retire after all. Four years later, the sexton swore this time retirement was real and reached out again to Rob. His only hesitation when taking the municipal job was how much interaction he would have with families because at the funeral home he would see and help at least four families each day.

> When I came here, I wasn't sure how much of that I would get. I knew it was a good move for me financially and for my family with the benefits. I meet enough families and feel that I'm helping them through a similar process, just not meeting them at the house when grandma passed away.

I asked him, like I did the other cemetery managers, why he stays in this job. "There was some empathy in my family I guess," explaining that his dad was a priest and his mom was a nurse.

> When I was in school, I got a degree in journalism, so part of that training is listening, picking up things … So, part of my success as a funeral director was being able to sit down with families in a really tough spot for them and ease their fears a bit.

Meeting families, he explained, is tricky. You must be able to read the room, almost predicting what families are thinking through their grief. "Being exposed to an actual dead body was a test, and it didn't bother me so much. I don't take the pain away; that's impossible. I try to make it easier for them to grieve in a healthy way."

Concluding Remarks

There is no playbook for being a cemetery sexton. Each family is different. Each cemetery is different. Natural hazards could impede operations. Budgets are tight. Rules and regulations must be followed. Telling people no is difficult enough, and couple that with when people are mourning. Sextons are multi-faceted individuals who have to be a jack of all trades. This chapter highlighted various aspects of empathy and how sextons learn as they go. Each cemetery manager dealt with grief in their own way – slamming people into boards during a hockey game, enjoying a glass of wine, working out, crying in the car, taking a breather during the day. Nothing is right for everyone.

Empathy and Beyond 77

Each response is a coping strategy for the sextons. Professionalism could come across as detachment and is a learned reaction to a hard situation, whereas a connected response to grief is based on active engagement with the situation (Morse et al., 1992). Neither is right or wrong – it depends. As a public service encounter, though, there could be more at stake in the cemetery given the extra layer of grief involved.

Said Jessica McGroarty from Edgartown, Massachusetts of this tension:

> I hate to say I have to keep that barrier up because I can't sit here and hold somebody's hand and cry for an hour with them. I try not to come off as cold. I try to be as helpful as possible, but I try to remain as professional as possible. I don't want details. If I get details, I am just gonna sit at my desk and cry all day.

References

Edgette J.J. (1999). "Now I lay me down to sleep …": Symbols and their meaning on children's gravemarkers. *Children's Folklore Review*, 22(1), 7–24.

Edlins, M. & Dolamore, S. (2018). Ready to serve the public? The role of empathy in public service education programs. *Journal of Public Affairs Education*, 24(3), 300–320.

Grandey, A.A. (2000). Emotion regulation in the workplace: A new way to conceptualize emotional labor. *Journal of Occupational Health Psychology*, 5(1), 95–110.

Guy, M.E. (2019). Expanding the toolbox: Why the citizen-state encounter demands it. *Public Performance & Management Review*, DOI: https://doi.org/10.1080/15309576.2019.1677255

Guy, M.E. & Mastracci, S. (2018). Making the affective turn: The importance of feelings in theory, praxis and citizenship. *Administrative Theory & Praxis*, 40(4), 281–288.

Haveman, M. (1999). A sociohistorical analysis of children's gravestones. *Illness, Crisis & Loss*, 7(3), 266–286.

Hsieh, C.W., Yang, K., & Fu, K.-J. (2011). Motivational bases and emotional labor: Assessing the impact of public service motivation. *Public Administration Review*, 72, 241–251.

Lauterbach, S.S. (2003). Phenomenological silence surrounding infant death. *International Journal for Human Caring*, 7(2), 38–43.

Morse, J.M., Bottorff, J., Anderson, G., O'Brien, B. & Solberg, S. (1992). Beyond empathy: expanding expressions of caring. *Journal of Advanced Nursing*, 17(7), 809–821.

Wiseman, T. (1996). A concept analysis of empathy. *Journal of Advanced Nursing*, 23(6), 1162–1167.

7 Cemetery Potpourri

You know what the best question is in the world? When you just introduce yourself to someone who has no idea about you. The question is, "Hey Bill, what do you do for a living?" And it's like what do you say? Well, I just get it out of the way – I'm a grave digger. They go, "What?!" Then my wife looks at me and goes, no he's the director of cemeteries. They go, there's no such job. I tell them, you got no idea.

(Bill Bibby, cemetery director, City of Charlotte)

In this chapter, I highlight stories and practices that did not neatly fit into the chapters above based on my data coding. I wanted to share these stories because I believe they highlight the myriad challenges cemetery managers face that perhaps their colleagues in other departments do not. The stories also give researchers a place to explore these concepts further either in cemetery management or within public service in general by finding those administrators who often go overlooked (like coroners, perhaps).

Historic Preservation

Kelly Thomas, project manager for historic burying grounds in the City of Boston, oversees 16 historical cemeteries. Kelly has a degree in historic preservation from Boston University and saw a job ad for her position in 2000. The ad was intriguing, she said, because it called for someone with her degree and expertise. Her job requires knowledge not only in historic preservation, but as a municipal employee she also must bear in mind procurement laws, grant writing, contracting ethics, and general municipal rules and regulations. This all gets a bit trickier when historical preservation is concerned because the contractors need experience in that area in addition to general work that might need to be done.

For example, some historic cemeteries she oversees date to the 1600s so there might not be ample parking, electricity, or utilities. Some of the cemeteries are in crowded downtown spaces so traditional equipment cannot navigate the area.

Cemetery Potpourri 79

For me, the sites that I manage, they're old burying grounds so many of them are not accessible by vehicle because maybe it's an acre site, and the ones from the 1600s they didn't drive in there so it's not like these big cemeteries that there are today that cars drive in.

Historical cemeteries in Boston fall under not only city law but also federal historic preservation guidelines, landmark district policies, and historical commission practices. There are many layers of government, then, that Kelly needs to listen to in her role. Not only that, she also deals with property law – who owns the headstones or grave markers? Headstones placed in the 1700s, for instance, were private property then but now fall under the city's purview.

I'm not a genealogist, but descendants from one person in 1700s, there's certainly hundreds if not thousands. Who are they? I don't know. We don't get approval from people because it would just be absolutely impossible. Would you have to get all thousands of them? We have let family groups if they want to do conservation work just to maintain or stop deterioration of the site, then we let them do that. But nobody can make any changes because we don't let people place new monuments or memorials.

It is no surprise that historical preservation is an expensive endeavor. Kelly said the department gets about $140,000 annual budget, so to supplement she applies for historic preservation grants and receives money from nighttime tours of some historic sites. The tour company works on a contract basis, and funding is returned to the city. The tours are a way to slow down – not prevent – some landscape erosion from taking place. When people walk on the grass, it will naturally become damaged and possibly die if not replenished and replaced. "Anyone who walks there is going to contribute to landscape erosion, so we want them to contribute to maintenance fees," said Kelly about the tours. Indeed, one cemetery property is on the popular Freedom Trail, historical sites throughout Boston that relate to the country's founding, so extra care is needed there because it is a popular tourist destination.

She told me about several projects she was working on related to conservation and preservation. She mentioned one in which they won a preservation award that involved stopping landscape erosion in the city's most-visited historic cemetery site. The idea was to widen the pedestrian path, which seems like an easy enough task. The challenge, though, was the cemetery is small and there is no space for vehicle access. The contractor had to hand-pour concrete, dig new fencing holes by hand, and work closely with an archaeologist to monitor what was being dug up. "It might've been my favorite project," Kelly said.

When we spoke in 2019, a big project she was working on involved grave marker conservation of 140 slate stones. She explained that slate naturally

80 *Cemetery Potpourri*

splits, so part of the challenge is to see if the crack is simple enough to repair or if the entire marker needs to be replaced. "A common problem is that they break at the point where they go underground. You could just reset them, but the epitaph would be covered. Sometimes you can find the bottom but sometimes you can't because it's completely underground." Her team can attach the stones back if they can find the exact spot, but sometimes it is easier to go for full replacement.

Despite the intense popularity of many Boston cemeteries, "I don't know that people know if I exist. They figure that someone takes care of it. I think they don't realize its more complicated than they imagined," Kelly said about her role in historic preservation. For her, the historical aspects of the cemeteries are some of her favorite parts of the job – she gets to deep dive into American lore. Paul Revere. John Hancock. Samuel Adams. These are just some of the notable historical figures buried in some of the city's cemeteries. "I feel it's a thrill to be involved even on the periphery with people like that."

Networking is Key

Stan Rogers, the cemetery director in Rome, Georgia, has a degree in public administration from the University of Georgia, and his research project was mausoleums. That work directly translated into the opening in 2013 of a $3 million mausoleum project in Myrtle Hill Cemetery within the city. Why? Well, the city cemeteries were beginning to run out of spaces. He said in the early 2000s there were no more spaces to sell at Myrtle Hill Cemetery. "I would think, 'I wonder how other cities handle things like this?' "

He called the Georgia Municipal Association and worked with them to obtain a list of all the cities in the state with certified cemetery operations. He reached out and asked people if they would support starting a Georgia Municipal Cemetery Association. "So back in 2007, we had a meeting in Macon in a tractor shed. It was at the public works. It was in a big old building they called the tractor shed." More than 100 people came to that initial meeting, and from there the organization became official in 2008. Stan served as the first president for four years, and the organization is still going strong with large statewide conferences and regional workshops each year.

> I would be confronted with these different things that are happening, and I wondered what other cities would do in a situation like this. And now we've got a network, a very good network. Every meeting we have interesting topics.

A lot of this job is trial by fire, preparing for the unexpected. Stan told me he was a few months into his director position when some people came into the cemetery and knocked over 85 historical monuments, most of which were

Cemetery Potpourri   81

more than a century old. Some that were damaged belonged to family members of Woodrow Wilson, including his first wife and her relatives. Her marker did not break because it was so big, Stan said, but those of her family were severely damaged. He said:

> My crew worked 16 hours a day for seven days and restored everything that we could, and the ones that we could not restore we brought to the Rome Monument Company here to have them rebuild and painstakingly restore [the markers]. We didn't want to replace anything, so my group just restored everything and restored them back up that wasn't broken and stuff. That's a big job with those big monuments, and you have to set them back up. I hadn't been the director probably six months, and I found myself in the back of Channel 42 WCBS in Atlanta. I found myself in the back of their live truck watching myself give interviews and tell news reporters from all over the place what happened, what we are going to do to fix it, and everything I was allowed to tell them.

From something major such as a national television news story to fire ants and flower beds, Stan knew a network was important to success in the job. Now through the Georgia Municipal Cemetery Association (GMCA), there are connections for cemetery managers and related public servants (grounds keepers, public works directors, parks and recreation employees, etc.) throughout Georgia and beyond.

> You have to figure out what to do all at once, and so the more I can get them (his crew) involved in the office, the more I can get them involved in the GMCA and networking with people running the GMCA, now that'll better prepare them and the cemetery won't have to go through a drastic change of rules and how we do this, because we're always changing. But there's always still a certain way you're supposed to talk to families. There's a certain way you're supposed to conduct yourself. One of the things I've always tried to tell them is back when I first started a family walked in and I said, "How are y'all doing today?" The lady started crying and said she wasn't doing too good because she just lost her husband. If they walk in here, they probably aren't having a great day.

Similarly, Christopher Cooke from Evansville, Indiana told me "I forget how many times I've held the title president" because pushing and developing a professional network for cemetery managers is critical. Christopher has been president of the Indiana Cemetery Association, and vice chairman of the Indiana State Board of Funeral and Cemetery Services. He has training from the International Cemetery, Cremation, and Funeral Association (ICCFA), the leading cemetery education and networking group in the US.

82   *Cemetery Potpourri*

I used to think that you could hide from it and turn it on and off like a switch. The older I got, I realized some people lead and others play a role. I'm one of those people who just leads.

Beyond networking for cemetery management, Christopher also shared how he likes to connect with people who also have an interest in history. He served as past president of the county's historical society and was a history major in college. "To be able to be around history every day and love what you do, that's some of the happiest stuff."

Bill Bibby from Charlotte also understands the power of networking and teaching. He said many new sextons sometimes are thrown into the field without a lot of training (depending, of course, upon the city and its succession planning practices) and might not know where to look to get problems resolved. In his home he keeps a library of books related to cemetery management, and he sees the power of networking in sharing those ideas with others. He often speaks at state and national conferences, and he prefers open forums because it gives him a chance to share knowledge related to specific topics of interest to the audience rather than a prepared slide-based presentation. Networking, then, is a constant necessity for sextons facing issues and expanding their knowledge bases.

Death is a Reality – So Why is it a Secret?

Returning to Bill Bibby, he shared a story with me about the friendships he has made in his role – sometimes unexpected ones. He told me a story of a time he worked for another city and the father of a 3-year-old girl was making arrangements for her death. She was terminally ill, and the father knew she was going to die.

He called me the night she was dying in his arms, and he called me. He called *me*. I'm like, that's the kind of friendship you get. How ironic I say about life, three months later they were pregnant again. Those stories are funky, too. Nobody wants to talk to us until something happens. We're not recognized until something happens.

Some people in my study spoke about the need to talk more openly about death. This makes sense as death itself has become more commodified and transactional (Sloane, 2018). In the internet world, this could be changing with digital memorials or death cafes. Death Café is an organization founded in 2011 in the United Kingdom that encourages people to gather over tea or coffee and talk about death – and thus living (Death Café, 2019). Gatherings such as these, or even discussions within the family, normalize death and open the door for more pre-planning at cemeteries.

Cemetery Potpourri 83

"I didn't know anything about the death process, and I learned that quickly," said Melissa Haynes of Ruidoso, New Mexico.

I don't think people have any idea about cemeteries except for that's where you put your grandparents when they die, and you're a kid when it happens. When you have to do it yourself, people have no clue it's going to cost $1,800 to bury someone. People don't know that someone else has to go out and dig the grave, and I can't let you open it yourself ... I just kind of wish people knew the rules and regulations in place are not because we're mean people. It's because there's rules and regulations, and I have no say so over the matter. I'm just the messenger.

For Tish Hopkins, cemetery supervisor in Concord, Massachusetts, the job is both about learning and solving puzzles. She started at the cemetery at 17, and "I had never even mowed a lawn before. At first I thought this was a little weird because these people are all dead." A few weeks into her job, Tish had to dig a grave, and "at that time I didn't grasp how big of a deal it was honestly." Her plan was to stay until she turned 18, but her boss at the time left and she stepped into the position. She started as a laborer, then equipment operator, and onto supervisor. "Grave digger isn't something that was typically thought of as a career path. I don't know how people find this job."

She has stayed at the cemetery this long because:

it answers questions. It's so much mystery as to what goes on at a cemetery. People don't know, and people don't want to know necessarily. It's not something that you research. You just kind of drive away in your car. You leave your loved one in a casket on a lowering device at some cemetery, and you trust that whoever is driving over there to fill the grave or lower your family member or friend into the ground is going to do it with some kind of respect and caring. I find it amazing that people trust us to be that person. I've thought about it. When I go to a funeral now, and for many years, when I go to a funeral, I stay. I wait. I talk to the people who are working there. I want to know that what's happening gets done.

Tish oversees the popular Sleepy Hollow cemetery where many notable authors and other historical figures are buried. She also has a personal connection to the town, having grown up there. Since she began working for the cemetery, Tish has buried her parents and a boyfriend.

I don't do anything differently for them than any other person. Every grave I dig is, you want to make sure it's the best it can possibly be. I lived in this town my whole life. All my coworkers think I'm kind of anal, but I don't care. I take care of this person like their family would do

84　*Cemetery Potpourri*

it themselves. I say my job is like an opportunity. I can help these family members, the people who come to me in the worst time of their lives, not to grieve with them but to help them through their process.

Cemetery Boards

Another interesting topic that emerged was the role of cemetery boards. Most were advisory, appointed by a municipal elected official, while some others were directly elected themselves. Many board members had no experience with cemetery management but instead had political connections or an interest in volunteering. Some boards had more power than others regarding cemetery decisions. This was not an express focus of my research, but as I spoke to more sextons it became clear this is an avenue that needs further study given the power and governance differentials. Cemetery boards are citizen advisory boards, and there is a tension in the scholarly literature regarding their overall effectiveness (Houghton, 1988). Looking specifically at that kind of board, in conjunction with "friends of the cemetery" volunteer organizations could be a fruitful stream of inquiry. I include here some basic findings from my data regarding these boards.

Sometimes, citizen advisory boards are perceived as a hindrance to governance process rather than a help (Houghton, 1988) and this seemed to manifest in the Town of Chapel Hill. In Chapter 4, I shared the story from Debra Lane of how the cemetery board was not consulted before the town officials sold cemetery land for affordable housing. Members quit *en masse*. Debra told me the board was created in 2009 with a goal of fixing up the town's cemeteries and listening to concerns from residents about the cemeteries. "Nobody is interested in the cemetery because the town has so many boards and so much land that other departments want to do something with the land, and the cemetery is way down on the bottom of the list." Debra would attend the meetings to answer any questions from board members or elected officials, but after the land sale board members became angry. "The board felt that why are we a board when you're not listening to us? Anything they put forward to the council took forever." June 2019 was the board's last meeting, and nobody even showed up. "I believe they did not want to serve anymore because of the way they were treated by the town."

It is perhaps not surprising, then, that Arnstein (1969) called citizen advisory boards "rubberstamp" (p. 218), token forms of citizen participation in governing processes. Ideally, citizen advisory boards are bodies that give advice to leaders and decision makers because members have expertise, but even internal politics can stymie the best-intentioned members (Brown, 1955). Given many board members are political appointees, the roles are merely advisory and the rubberstamps of favored policies or practices. Arnstein (1969) notes when board members become aware of these token roles, they might begin to fight back by demanding more of a say – or quitting in the case of Chapel Hill.

True to form, no two boards in my research were alike. Some had officials elected directly to the cemetery board, while others had appointed members serving fixed terms. For instance, Valerie Fox in Lincoln, Massachusetts said their town has an elected cemetery commission. "The commissioners tend to stay for a long time, which I think is fantastic because they're very knowledgeable and they know a lot about us." One member, she told me, has served for 25 years so has institutional memory of changes to the town's cemeteries. Another member has expertise in horticulture so "she will say create a bank of ferns and call it Fern Way ... She will be very careful about maintaining all the trees in great condition and the plantings, making sure they're native plantings." A third member really knows the town's history, with his family dating back at least 100 years in Lincoln.

Commissioners are elected to provide ideas on maintenance and give overall policy guidance for the four town cemeteries. Valerie said they also need to be forward thinking, knowing if more land is needed or being responsive to industry trends. For instance, when the town opened a new section of the Lexington Road Cemetery, the commission wanted a solar-powered shed, which allows for charging of maintenance equipment. A majority of the commission's responsibilities is creating policies, and if a person wants a variance to those rules, they need to appeal to the board. "I perform on their behalf" when implementing cemetery policies, Valerie said. Another city board could not supersede their decisions. "In this town, like say we had a leash law. We don't actually have a leash law ... but the cemetery commission could impose that because they're elected. The Board of Selectmen couldn't overrule them."

Citizen boards or committees often vary in scope, power, and domain but a general common characteristic is ideally to provide expertise on the selected domain (Williamson & Fung, 2004). Schaller (1964) traces the popularity of citizen boards to the National Housing Act of 1954, which required organizations seeking federal funding to have elements of citizen engagement. Schaller (1964) argues the most important function of such boards is to serve as a mediator between elected officials, bureaucratic experts, and the public – sometimes with all groups speaking different disciplinary languages. These boards and committees fail, though, when they do not represent the public but instead are filled with political favorites.

Craig Hudson of Auburn, Washington said the cemetery board meets every other month. "They don't write policy. They're kind of like a sounding board. I'll bounce ideas off them." He told me a story of a family that violated cemetery policy by ordering a large headstone in materials that did not fit the requirements. Cemetery rules only allow bronze or granite stones because marble, sandstone, and concrete:

isn't going to hold up to the test of time. The family, without asking, all of a sudden there's this big monument they wanted to have delivered here and it wasn't the standard. They wanted to talk to the board, so it was nice to have that backup. It was very helpful in that instance.

His board members include the former cemetery supervisor, a manager for Boeing, and a former state senator, among others. But decisions related to the cemetery, Craig said, are ultimately his.

We have a parks board, tree board, museum board. I think as we get bigger, I think it just makes sense to have a board specific to a certain department, I guess. I've heard where the cemetery falls under the parks board, and that can include different departments, so you get bogged down with things that don't really pertain to the cemetery and get kind of tiring. I think it's wise to have a board that pertains just to the cemetery. I tried to get people on the board who have a vested interest because they have loved ones here.

Denise Nestor of Norwell, Massachusetts told me the town's cemetery board has seen some changes and flux. The town's elected selectmen appoint members to the cemetery board, and the board's main tasks are enforcing cemetery rules and regulations. The board is basically her backup, similar to Craig's, but there was some tension when one member could not seem to enforce rules or regulations. "He was trying to protect his nest, shall we say," because he has a daughter buried in a town cemetery. That caused some friction on the board and led to some resignations. "It's taken a year, but we are all on the same page now." A goal of Denise's is to have someone in the funeral industry serve as a board member to bring that expertise.

Connie Goedert's cemetery commission in Queensbury, New York operates differently as well. "They get a third of every lot that's sold. That goes into a different account for perpetual care. If I need a lawnmower, it doesn't come out of my budget. It comes out of the cemetery commission." Each member is appointed by the town board for three years. The commission leader has long roots in the town, with Connie telling me the woman's father sold back some of his land to the town for the cemetery. "She grew up behind the cemetery, so she's always taken an interest in it." The commission meets monthly and like others focuses on policy development and implementation.

In sum, the cemetery boards either play an active or passive role, occupying potentially varied rungs on Arnstein's (1969) ladder of participation. The boards that included people with more expertise and knowledge about the municipality seemed more active based on my data. As noted, more research is needed to look deeper into the roles of these boards and "Friends Of" organizations that are nonprofits supporting cemetery operations.

Cemetery Potpourri

This last section offers short stories I simply thought were touching, neat, or a little strange and wanted to share in this volume. While sextons are public servants dealing with many of the same challenges as counterparts in the city, these stories are likely unique to the cemetery. I organize these as bulleted stories so I ask the reader to go with me while telling these tales of the crypts.

Don Price, Retired, City of Orlando

- "It's a weird profession. It really is." He has had three people commit suicide inside Greenwood Cemetery. "One I put my finger in the guy's brain to keep the blood from shooting out." The police arrived with guns drawn asking where the weapon was. Don explained the situation to the officer, and the person sadly passed away on the way to the hospital.
- He had a family fighting over the death of a baby. The father was Muslim, and the mother was Christian. "He wanted the baby sent to Mecca, she didn't. She had the baby buried without telling him because if the dug the baby up it's against the law. You get this stuff all the time."
- "I had a lady one day wanting me to dig up her grandmother to cut her finger off to get the ring. And I'm like, I'm not doing that. You need to get a court order."

Rob Jones, Anchorage, Alaska

- Before joining the city, Rob worked for a funeral home for eight years. Part of that role involved operating the crematory. Prior to 1964, he said, people who wanted to be cremated were shipped out of state, cremated, then shipped back home because there was no crematory in the state. This sometimes meant people forgot to pick up cremains or simply did not pick them up, leaving a backlog. One of his jobs before leaving his funeral home job was the catalog cremains left at the funeral home. Fast forward to 2017 when he helped a daughter bury her parents cremains in the family niche in the burial wall. The plaque had three names – mom, dad, and a boy who died in 1964. That urn, though, was not in the niche. The boy, this woman's brother, died at the age of 12 in a plane crash. Using another plane, her father found the wreckage and thus the bodies of his son and pilot.
- "The parents were so traumatized then that after cremation, they didn't do anything about it. They couldn't bring themselves to pick up the urn. That's not an uncommon story. That's a hard thing to do," Rob explained. Rob mentioned to the daughter/sister his prior work cataloging remains, and when he returned to his office he called his old funeral home. Sure

88 *Cemetery Potpourri*

enough, the employees there were able to find the name – and the urn. "A month later we put the boy in the niche with his parents more than 50 years later. It was awesome."

Connie Goedert, Queensbury, New York

- When her kids graduated from school, Connie herself went back to school to obtain a degree in mortuary science. Before that, she worked in Emergency Medical Services (EMS) so knew many of the local funeral directors. "My dad passed away when he was just 50, and I thought I always could do better than what he got from the funeral director." So she worked in town as a funeral director for 12 years before transitioning to work for the Town of Queensbury.
- In 2018, Connie ran for and was elected a coroner of Warren County. Her term is four years, and in her role she works with unattended deaths, so people not under a doctor's care, a suicide, accident, or any questionable death. "It's pretty interesting. It's just another thing I always wanted to do. It's very interesting, plus you're dealing with families at the worst time in their lives. And I feel that I can't fix the situation, but I can help them with what they' re going through. I love it."

Tricia Neal, Somerset, Kentucky

- "So there's this Bluegrass musician who was buried in an unmarked grave here, and nobody really knew about it because he kind of faded from glory." The musician turned out to be Leonard Rutherford, part of the duo who wrote the original version of the song "Man of Constant Sorrow." Rutherford fell on hard times and died alone, buried in the unmarked grave. Neal said a man from a neighboring town came to her when doing some research of Rutherford's musical partner Dick Burnett. "He had a clue the other half of the duo was buried here. I'm like, I don't have a record of him." When she dug into the records, turns out the name was there but no indication of a headstone.
- The researcher then paid for a grave marker for Rutherford. "We built this whole event around marking his grave, and it turned out to be the most awesome thing ever. We found this guy's long-lost family from all over the country who traveled to come here. It turns out a lot of them were into Bluegrass music, so that was neat. We had this whole pickin' festival out there by his grave, and they played some of his old songs, and they played some newer songs. There was a guy playing the spoons. Who plays the spoons anymore?! That was probably the highlight of my time here was pulling that together because there were just so many neat aspects of it."

Photo 7.1 People playing spoons during a festival.
Source: Photo courtesy Tricia Neal, Somerset, Kentucky.

Neal Currie, Bangor, Maine

- A lumber baron from the 1800s is buried in a city cemetery. He was wealthy but divorced. "She wanted half his money. He said she could have it when he was buried six feet under. He was buried above ground so she got nothing."

Melissa Haynes, Ruidoso, New Mexico

- "I had a gentleman whose mother passed away. She was buried on a Saturday, and he called me on a Monday and said someone went out and destroyed the roses on my mother's grave. I am just mortified. We live in a really decent little town here. I leave my door unlocked. I leave my keys in my car. I sent my guys to look. We have a huge population of deer that just roam around town. The deer ate every single rose … on the grave. It was kind of funny, but in an odd, weird, gross way. I was like, of course why didn't I think of that! I was ready to fight someone because they cut this man's mother's roses off his grave."

90   *Cemetery Potpourri*

Bob Nelson, Deadwood, South Dakota

- "We do burials year-round. We'll figure out a way to thaw the ground in the winter. There's a way to. You throw a heat blanket down on the ground. It's a ground-thawing blanket. The frost here, typically by about February is probably four feet in the ground. It's got hot water tubes that run through it, so there's a portable boiler that holds water and it heats it. It runs on electricity or diesel fuel and pumps water through the coils like a radiator, and it sits on the ground and it just pulls the frost out of the ground."
- (I included this anecdote because as someone raised in Florida and who has lived in basically tropical climates, the idea of a blanket that pulls frost from the ground blew my mind. Ask Bob. He can tell you I was amazed and did not have words on the phone for a while.)

Chris Waite, Billings, Montana

- "A lot of people, there's a stigma associated with cemetery, so they're kind of fearful coming here. Our cemetery is a beautiful space. It's like a park how we have it, and we have so much rich history here. We have a few people tied to the Western expansion, relatives of Buffalo Bill. I wish that people, just the public in general felt more comfortable approaching the cemetery and could appreciate the history of the site as well. I know most of us have that association with funerals and family members that have passed on."

Dawn Ubelaker, Nome, Alaska

- "In the middle of doing all this data transfer and map upgrade, I came across a name. There was something not quite right. The date of birth or date of death didn't match the information listed in the book, so I did more research."
- She did some research and came across his obituary from the 1900s. He was a Greek immigrant and took a sled dog team to a nearby outpost. "It's like a full day sled dog ride to the outpost."
- The obituary, which was front-page news, said the man was missing for a few days because of harsh winter blizzards, and people only found out because one of the dogs showed back up alone in Nome. People said, "okay that's not a good sign, let's go find him" once the weather was safer. People found the man frozen to his sled. The dogs had chewed off their harnesses and began eating the man's remains. "It was four or five days later that he was found half devoured and frozen to his sled."
- Now Dawn wonders, "are some of the dogs that I'm catching and putting in our shelter, are they descendants of the dogs who ate that guy?"

Cemetery Potpourri 91

(Remember Dawn is both the animal control office and cemetery manager, so this really is a story of her worlds colliding.)

Denise Nestor, Norwell, Massachusetts

* When we spoke, Denise had been in her position for nearly a year and a half. How did she get there? "It's really kind of funny. I was out on medical leave for a massive stroke. It's all good. I'm here. Because I was out for one-and-a-half years, they had to fill my position, which is completely understandable. So when I came back, they were like, 'What are we going to do with you?' This was dumped in my lap. At first, I resented it, but now I love it. That's pretty much how I got into it."

Mark Thompson, Paducah, Kentucky

* He told me a story of someone called Speedy buried in a city cemetery. "There was a black funeral home back in the day, this was before the 1937 flood, that tested their Egyptian elixir embalming technique. They kept Speedy in a closet there, but during the '37 flood, Speedy went downstream, and they found him. They finally ended up burying him in Oak Grove."
* I had to Google this story, and the person was named Charles "Speedy" Atkins who died in 1928 as a pauper. His corpse was propped in the funeral home, and Speedy became a tourist attraction who onlookers gawked at (*Chicago Sun-Times*, 1994). He was a tobacco worker known for his speed, thus the nickname. He drowned in the Ohio River, and the funeral director tried his new embalming technique. The man displayed Speedy's body, and Speedy was finally buried nearly 66 years after his death (NKAA, 2019).

Concluding Remarks

Going into this project, I almost expected the sextons to tell me all these wild and crazy stories. While I did get some of those, most of the tales were about public management issues – union workers, grounds maintenance, leadership, records management, deed recording, equipment purchasing, budget, and finance. Not that the job is boring; surely that is not the case. But there is much more that is routine than meets the eye. That said, the cemetery is complicated because they are often so large and have historic components that come with another set of managerial challenges. Add in familial grief, and the job becomes that much more complex. At the end of the day, though, sextons are public servants trying to do the best job for the public they can.

92 *Cemetery Potpourri*

References

Arnstein, S.R. (1969). A ladder of citizen participation. *Journal of the American Institute of Planners*, 35(4), 216–224.

Brown. D.S. (1955). The public advisory board as an instrument of government. *Public Administration Review*, 15(3), 196–204.

Chicago Sun-Times (1994). Embalmed "Speedy" is laid to rest – finally. Retrieved from: https://web.archive.org/web/20150329082552/www.highbeam.com/doc/1P2–4241651.html

Death Café (2019). What is a death café? Retried from: https://deathcafe.com/what/

Houghton, D.G. (1988). Citizen advisory boards: Autonomy and effectiveness. *American Review of Public Administration*, 18(3), 283–296.

NKAA (2019). Charles "Speedy" Atkins. Retrieved from: https://nkaa.uky.edu/nkaa/items/show/1255

Schaller, L.E. (1964). Is the citizen advisory committee a threat to representative government? *Public Administration Review*, 24(3), 175–179.

Sloane, D.C. (2018). *Is the cemetery dead?* Chicago: University of Chicago Press.

Williamson, A. & Fung, A. (2004). Public deliberation: Where are we and where can we go? *National Civic Review*, 93(4), 3–15.

8 Concluding Remarks

Cemeteries are historic places. Movers and shakers are buried there, people who started the community.

(Ted Dudley, Bureau of Cemeteries manager, City of Norfolk, Virginia)

Sloane (2018) pointedly asks if the cemetery is dead before deftly tracing the history of funeral and memorial practices throughout US history. His question comes given a transition to more cremations versus traditional burials, public versus private memorials, and passive versus active responses to these and other funeral industry changes. He concludes that the cemetery is not dead but changing.

Corporatization, technology, money, and pop culture changed how people relate to the cemetery, taking the spaces from tranquil public parks to spots where someone is put (Bry, 2019). Yet the sextons in this research, like some in Bry's (2019) article, are finding new ways to bring people to the cemetery, to bring back the park-like atmosphere that encourages walking, jogging, sitting, picnicking, learning.

Tonja Walls-Davis, cemetery division manager in Austin, Texas, has a background in both the healthcare and death care industries. She is a licensed funeral director and embalmer. When she began college, she was a nursing major, but:

the mortuary science department was right next door on the same floor, so I found myself just wandering down there all the time because it was interesting what they were doing. Finally, I started my clinicals in nursing and just didn't feel like it was for me. I researched, and then I found my calling. It was in mortuary science.

Her uncle was the founder of a funeral home in Grand Rapids, Michigan, and many of her family members still work in the industry today. She started at a small funeral home but eventually worked for a larger corporation then applied when the opening in Austin came up in 2016. She manages five city

94 *Concluding Remarks*

Photo 8.1 Olympic Memorial.

cemeteries and two family-owned cemeteries also under the city's purview. Despite her experience in the funeral industry, she never planned an interment – the funeral homes stopped when it reached that point. She also had to learn to handle departmental politics and elected official politics as a public servant.

Concluding Remarks 95

Prior to her joining the city, cemeteries were contracted out but brought back into city operations in 2013, so the position was three years new when she took over.

"[City officials] wanted to bring that personal care back in house. This is some of the city's most favored assets in the cemetery. This is Austin's history," she said. Together, the cemeteries make up about 200 acres, and they do various public-facing events to bring people in to learn that Austin history.

Along with those new walking tours, Tonja told me talking to families was both old hat and new.

> You think by the time the family reaches the cemetery, a lot of the real hard part is done. I dealt with so much more on the funeral side of it. You deal with the initial shock. You deal with all of that from the funeral home end. That part of it has not been as bad. My uncle was a very good teacher, and he pretty much started his funeral home from the ground up. My degree is in psychology so that was part of it too. That kind of helped me understand what people were going through, the stages of grief, that kind of helped me, too. I always felt like, man I'm doing a service for people that not too many people can do. Like I always tell people here, and I always lived by this in the funeral industry, we only get one time to do this. Other professions, you get a do over. You only get one time to bury somebody. Even at the funeral, you only get one time to have that service, and that's the pressure that I've always put on my staff. You only get one time.

The sextons were generous with their time, explaining this unique public service role that seemingly goes unnoticed until something is needed or wrong. The cemetery is at once still and constantly moving – grass mowed, services, visitors, tourists, administrative work, public history, and so much more. Each person to whom I spoke was passionate about this work. Some had only just begun (I talked to one person who was a week into her position) while others spent nearly four decades in the role. The cemetery managers seemed happy to share their experiences with me, and now I with you.

"I love this job because of the compassionate standpoint and the fact that it's something that people really need, and it's a service I'm able to provide," said Dawn Ubelaker from Nome, Alaska. Many of the sextons felt the same way – they are public servants doing necessary jobs but have to go above and beyond other municipal roles because the grief element is nearly ever-present. Said Ken Carroll of Plainfield Township, Illinois,

> We don't have secrets out here. The amount of shock on people's faces when I tell them we try to treat everyone here like they're small town

96 *Concluding Remarks*

rural, like they're family. Funeral homes are a one and done thing, but we're going to see these people every day or every week.

If nothing else, I hope this book showcases the unsung public service roles, opening us up to a willingness to seek out and share these stories. There is a lot of lived experiences and uniqueness when we as scholars look for it. While there might be a push in public administration scholarship toward increasingly sophisticated quantitative methods and modeling, there is a beauty in asking someone why or how. These in-depth interviews created a space for me to tell some of those stories from managers that are so vital to our everyday understanding of the administrative state (Hummell, 1991).

As I began this research with a story from Don Price, the City of Orlando's retired sexton, it seems only fitting to conclude with some as well.

"I don't think anybody chooses it," he said about becoming a sexton.

> It happens. You're chosen. I don't think that you choose, you're chosen. When you look at the person, and you look at the families, it's all about the families. It's not anything to do with the money, the this, the that. It's all about the families. You're going to find that a lot of your sextons are chosen.

Don and I met for our interview in an Orlando dive bar called Big Daddy's. We were there on a weekday afternoon, and a small crowd was already gathered to drink, smoke, and talk. Don is an affable man, his white hair and some tattoos visible that day. City Commissioner Patty Sheehan described him in an article as "an elegant southern redneck gentleman" (Spies, 2017, para. 6). Talking with him, you can tell he misses the job but remains connected through his cemetery walking tours, doing videos with another UCF professor, and speaking throughout the community. But his heart, I believe, remains with the cemetery and the people there because if anyone knows their stories, it is Don.

> If I bury your child and if it means nothing to me, then I'm not human. I'm not human. It became very emotional that every time I buried someone, I took a part of you because that was your mom or that was your dad. That was your boyfriend or your husband that you don't even have the simple snuggles anymore. That was your life. If I did not take that with me home, then I wasn't human. I thought it would be more management, but it became more emotional where I would sit down and I would meet with you and I would talk with you, and I'd learn about you and I'd hear your story. It was amazing, no matter what it was, it was amazing.

Concluding Remarks 97

References

Bry, J. (2019). Public life after death: How six cemeteries are reclaiming their role as public spaces. Retrieved from: www.pps.org/article/how-six-cemeteries-are-reclaiming-their-role-as-public-spaces

Hummell, R.P. (1991). Stories managers tell: Why they are as valid as science. *Public Administration Review*, 51(1), 31–41.

Sloane, D.C. (2018). *Is the cemetery dead?* Chicago: University of Chicago Press.

Spies, M. (2017). A graveyard, and a caretaker, for victims of the Pulse massacre. Retrieved from: www.newyorker.com/news/news-desk/a-graveyard-and-a-caretaker-for-victims-of-the-pulse-massacre

Index

African-American burials 32–7, 41
author walk 52

burial, changes to 12, 32, 44, 65, 85, 93
burial season 1, 7, 90

cemetery ordinances 22, 51
Christianity 10, 21, 54, 87
citizen advisory boards 84
citizen engagement 85
City of Austin 1, 13, 41, 93, 95
City of Bangor 57–8, 69, 73, 89
City of Boston 13, 54, 78–80
City of Charlotte 14, 28, 33, 54, 74, 78, 82
City of Deadwood 47–8, 59, 90
City of Nome 1, 7, 19–20, 32, 56, 90, 95
City of Savannah 43, 51–2
City of Selma 34–7
Civil War 35, 56
Columbaria 12, 16, 31, 51
cremation 12, 16, 19, 23–5, 31–2, 41–4, 81, 87
cultural competence 2, 24, 30

dark tourism 6, 27, 35, 47
Death Café 82
deeds 13, 18, 27–8, 36, 91
digital records 19–20, 23, 25
disease prevention 10–12, 57

Eaton, Hubert 10–11
emotional labor 16, 64–8
empathy 7, 44, 62, 74–7
ethics 78
European ritual 50
extended land use 16, 22, 24

family cemetery 11–12, 15, 19, 22, 24–5, 35–8, 41–4, 52, 58
Forest Lawn Cemetery 10, 21, 72
Foucault 57–8
funeral cost 41–3, 83
funeral home 1, 3, 7, 19, 35, 41–2, 58, 71–2, 75–6, 87, 91, 93, 95

genealogy 9, 19, 34
Georgia Municipal Cemetery Association 80–1
ghost tour 6, 27, 54
GIS surveys 19, 25
green burial 12, 16
green space 38–9, 50
grounds maintenance 3, 11, 13, 15, 18, 22, 28, 34, 48, 52, 54, 58, 62, 74, 79, 85, 91

Halloween 53, 58–9
historic preservation 23, 25, 33, 35, 39, 47–8, 52, 58–9, 78–80

interment rights 21, 28, 43, 73, 94

Kentucky 13, 26–7, 33, 68, 88–9, 91

literary tourism 52
living history 26–8, 53–6
lot cards 19, 22–3

maps 19–20, 23, 25, 52
Memorial Day 54–8
Mount Auburn Cemetery 9–12
municipal politics 14–15, 84, 94

necrogeography 25

Index 99

networking 23, 80–2

parental loss 41, 69
Price, Don 2, 6, 13, 39, 54, 67, 87, 96
Pulse nightclub 2–3, 39–41

QR codes 23

records management 18–29, 34, 91
rural cemetery 9–11, 24–5, 33, 56, 96

self-care 13, 67
sexton defined 11–12

slave graves 14, 31, 33–9
Sleepy Hollow Cemetery 52, 83
social justice 30, 39, 41–2, 64
social media 3, 15–16, 23–4

thanatourism 50, 59
training 74–6, 81
traveling memorial 58

urban planning 9, 12, 44

Veterans Day 54, 58
virtual memorial 12

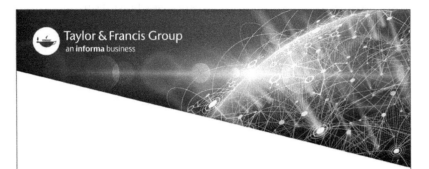

Taylor & Francis eBooks

www.taylorfrancis.com

A single destination for eBooks from Taylor & Francis with increased functionality and an improved user experience to meet the needs of our customers.

90,000+ eBooks of award-winning academic content in Humanities, Social Science, Science, Technology, Engineering, and Medical written by a global network of editors and authors.

TAYLOR & FRANCIS EBOOKS OFFERS:

A streamlined experience for our library customers

A single point of discovery for all of our eBook content

Improved search and discovery of content at both book and chapter level

REQUEST A FREE TRIAL
support@taylorfrancis.com

Ingram Content Group UK Ltd.
Milton Keynes UK
UKHW022110040523
421267UK00006B/53